THE EVERYTHING KIDS' MONSTERS BOOK

From ghosts, goblins, and gremlins to vampires, werewolves, and zombies—puzzles, games, and trivia guaranteed to keep you up at night

Shannon R. Turlington

Adams Media Corporation
Avon, Massachusetts

D0943537

EDITORIAL
Publishing Director: Gary M. Krebs
Managing Editor: Kate McBride
Copy Chief: Laura MacLaughlin
Acquisitions Editor: Cheryl Kimball
Development Editor: Christel A. Shea

PRODUCTION
Production Director: Susan Beale
Production Manager: Michelle Roy Kelly
Series Designer: Colleen Cunningham
Layout and Graphics: Brooke Camfield,
Colleen Cunningham, Rachel Eiben,
Daria Perreault
Cover Layout: Paul Beatrice, Frank Rivera

An Everything® Series Book.
Everything® is a registered trademark of Adams Media Corporation.

Published by Adams Media Corporation
57 Littlefield Street, Avon, MA 02322
www.adamsmedia.com

ISBN: 1-58062-657-2

Printed in the United States of America.

J I H G F E D C B A

Library of Congress Cataloging-in-Publication Data
Turlington, Shannon R.
The everything kids' monsters book : from ghosts, goblins, and
gremlins to vampires, werewolves, and zombies : puzzles, games, and
trivia guaranteed to keep you up at night / Shannon R. Turlington.
v.   cm.   —   (An Everything series book)
Includes bibliographical references and index.
ISBN 1-58062-657-2
1. Monsters—Juvenile literature. [1. Monsters.] II. Title. III. Everything series.
GR825 .T87 2002
001.944—dc21
2002004576

This publication is designed to provide accurate and authoritative information with regard to the subject matter covered. It is sold with the understanding that the publisher is not engaged in rendering legal, accounting, or other professional advice. If legal advice or other expert assistance is required, the services of a competent professional person should be sought.
— From a *Declaration of Principles* jointly adopted
by a Committee of the American Bar Association and a Committee of Publishers and Associations

Cover illustrations by Dana Regan.
Interior illustrations by Kurt Dolber, with contributions by Barry Littmann.
Puzzles by Beth Blair.

Puzzle Power Software by Centron Software Technologies, Inc. was used to create puzzle grids.

This book is available at quantity discounts for bulk purchases.
For information, call 1-800-872-5627.

See the entire *Everything*® series at *www.everything.com*.

CONTENTS

Introduction vii

Chapter 1

Vampires: The Best-Dressed Monsters / 1

Vampires Throughout History 2
   Ancient Vampires 2
   Slavic Vampires 3
   Real-Life Vampires? 4
   Dracula 4
Vampires Today 5
   Vampire Powers 6
   Becoming a Vampire 7
   Fighting Vampires 8
Vampire Diseases 9
`ACTIVITY` Make a Vampire Costume 10

Chapter 2

Werewolves and Other Shapeshifters / 11

What Is Shapeshifting? 12
   The First Shapeshifters 12
   Kinds of Shapeshifters 13
Werewolves: The Most Famous
   Shapeshifters 13

Why Wolves? 13
The First Werewolf 14
The Werewolf Trials 15
Werewolves among Us 16
   Identifying Werewolves 16
   Becoming a Werewolf 17
`ACTIVITY` Observe the Moon's Phases 20

Chapter 3

Ghosts and Other Things That Go Bump in the Night / 21

Spirits Who Stay Behind 22
   Ghosts Around the World 22
   Types of Ghosts 23
   Ghostly Theories 23
Tracking Down Ghosts 24
   Haunted Places 24
   Famous Hauntings 25
   Ghost Hunting 27
   Contacting Ghosts 28
   Putting Ghosts to Rest 29
Other Ghostly Monsters 30
   Poltergeists 31
   The Bogeyman 31
`ACTIVITY` Play the Haunted
House Game 32

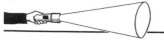 
Chapter 4
The Goblins Will Get You if You Don't Watch Out / 33

Those Gruesome Goblins 34
Fairies and Goblins 34
Goblins as Practical Jokers 35
Changelings 36
Types of Goblins 36
Gremlins 37
Trolls 37
Knockers 38
Bogies and Spriggans 38
Goblins: Where Bad Luck Comes From . . . 39
ACTIVITY Make Goblin Face Paint 41

Chapter 5
Zombies: The Walking Dead / 43

Called from the Grave 44
That Voodoo That You Do 44
Voodoo and Black Magic 45
Making a Zombie 46
The Zombie Powder 47
Zombie Cures and Prevention 47
Natural Causes 47
Hollywood Zombies 48
ACTIVITY Honor Your Ancestors 50

Chapter 6
Mummies: All Wrapped Up and Nowhere to Go / 51

What Are Mummies? 52
Accidental Mummies 52
Egyptian Mummies 53
How Mummies Are Made 54
The Mummy's Curse 55
King Tut 56
The Mummy and the *Titanic* 58
ACTIVITY Make an Apple Mummy 59

Chapter 7
Golems: Monsters Made of Clay / 61

Bringing Clay to Life 62
The First Golems 62
The Famous Golem of Prague 63
The Life of a Golem 64
How to Make a Golem 64
Why Golems Attack 65
Getting Rid of a Golem 67
Are These Golems? 67
Frankenstein's Monster 68
ACTIVITY Make Clay Monsters 69

 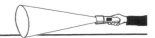
Chapter 8

Giants: Monsters of Myth / 71

Who Were the Giants? 72
   Giants in Greek Mythology 72
   Giants in Norse Mythology 74
   Giants in British Folklore 76
   Giants in Native American Folklore 80
Odious Ogres 80
ACTIVITY Write a Monster Story 81

Chapter 9

Bigfoot: The Mysterious Apeman / 83

Bigfoot Around the World 84
   Many Homes, One Monster 84
   Bigfoot, or the Sasquatch 85
   The Yeti 86
Who Is Bigfoot? 87
   Lack of Evidence 87
Putting Us On: Bigfoot Hoaxes 88
ACTIVITY Identify Animal Tracks 92

Chapter 10

Monsters of Lakes and Seas / 93

Lake Monsters 94
   Nessie, the Monster of Loch Ness 94
   Other Lake Monsters 95
   Living Dinosaurs 95
Sea Monsters 97
   Giant Squid and Octopi 97
   Giant Sharks 98
ACTIVITY Blow Monster Bubbles 100

Chapter 11

Weird Creatures / 101

Fearsome Animals 102
   El Chupacabra 102
   The Jersey Devil 103
   The Bunyip 104
Dragons 106
Chimeras 107
   The Manticore 108
ACTIVITY Create Your Own Monster 109

Chapter 12

Aliens: They Came from Outer Space / 111

Aliens among Us 112
   Ancient Astronauts 112
   Modern-Day Sightings 113
   Abducted! 114
   The Mysterious Men in Black 114
   A Case of Mistaken Identity 115
Types of Aliens 115
   Grays 116
   Reptoids 116
   Nordics 117
ACTIVITY Go Skywatching 118

Conclusion 119
Appendix A: Resources 121
   Books 121
   Web Sites 122
Appendix B: Glossary 123
Puzzle Answers 127
Index 131

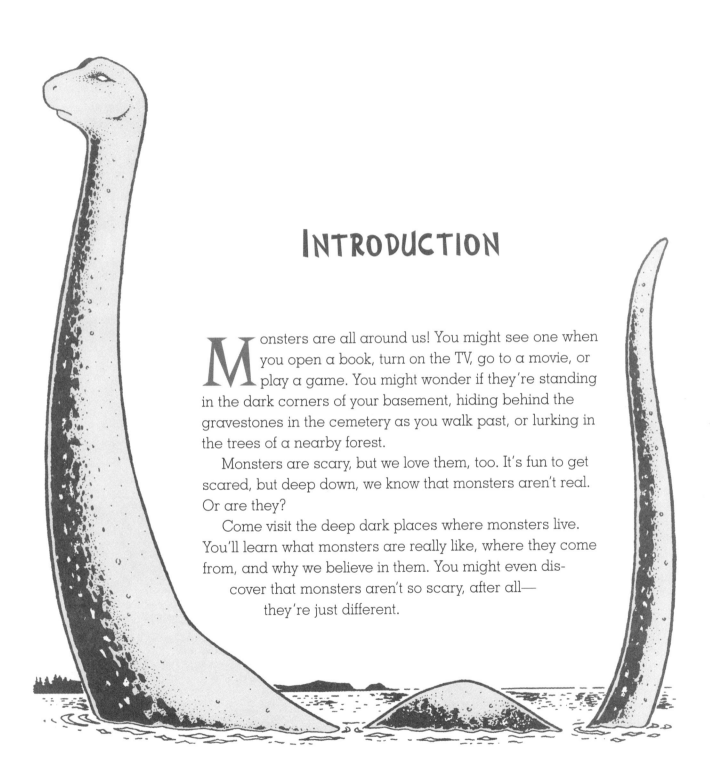

Introduction

Monsters are all around us! You might see one when you open a book, turn on the TV, go to a movie, or play a game. You might wonder if they're standing in the dark corners of your basement, hiding behind the gravestones in the cemetery as you walk past, or lurking in the trees of a nearby forest.

Monsters are scary, but we love them, too. It's fun to get scared, but deep down, we know that monsters aren't real. Or are they?

Come visit the deep dark places where monsters live. You'll learn what monsters are really like, where they come from, and why we believe in them. You might even discover that monsters aren't so scary, after all—they're just different.

CHAPTER 1

VAMPIRES: THE BEST-DRESSED MONSTERS

Vampires Throughout History

Of all monsters, vampires are the oldest and best known. People have told stories about vampires since ancient times, and vampire legends are known all over the world.

Like the vampires we hear about today, the first vampires rose from the grave to drink the blood of the living. Otherwise, they were very different. The ancient Greek vampire had the upper body of a woman and the lower body of a snake with wings. The Malaysian vampire was just a flying head that dragged its intestines behind it. In China, vampires were covered with green hair and had glowing red eyes.

These days, we think of vampires as looking just like people except for their very white skin and long sharp fangs. Vampires have evolved over thousands of years into the creatures we know today.

Ancient Vampires

We can trace vampire stories all the way back to ancient Babylon—5,600 years ago. The Babylonians told stories of vampire women who drank the blood of babies. Legends of vampires spread to the ancient empires of Egypt, Greece, and Rome.

The ancient Egyptians believed that garlic had healing powers. They put garlic in the mouths of the dead to keep them from rising from their graves. Garlic became a powerful weapon against vampires, and it remains one to this day.

As people moved into Europe and settled there, they brought their folk stories with them. Over the years, the stories changed a lot from the legends told in ancient times.

WORDS to KNOW

nosferatu: another name for a vampire, *nosferatu* comes from a Greek word that means "plague-carrier." One of the first vampire movies was called *Nosferatu*.

FUN FACT

Good Ol' Garlic

Garlic not only keeps vampires away, but it's also good for your health! Scientific studies have shown that eating a lot of garlic can lower blood pressure, reduce the risk of heart disease and cancer, and keep you from getting colds and flu.

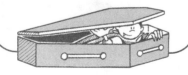

Q: Why do vampires hate arguments?

A: Because they make themselves cross.

 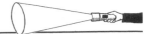
Slavic Vampires

The vampire stories we are most familiar with come from folktales told in eastern Europe, in the Slavic countries of Hungary, Serbia, and Romania. Belief in vampires reached its height in these countries in the early 1700s. At that time, many people thought vampires were real.

Peter Plogojowitz was the first person to be called a vampire in an official report. Peter lived in a small village in Serbia. A few weeks after his death in 1725, nine of the villagers died of a mysterious illness. Before they died, each claimed that Peter had visited them during the night. The villagers were convinced that Peter was a vampire. They dug up his grave, put a stake through his heart, and burned his body. The story of Peter the vampire spread throughout Europe and was even published in newspapers.

In 1732, an Austrian army medical officer reported another vampire epidemic in a Serbian village. In this village, seventeen villagers died during the space of a few weeks. Many people thought these villagers had become vampires. The dead villagers were dug up, and the medical officer reported that they did look like vampires. However, he might have thought that the normal **decomposition** of the bodies was a sign that the dead were actually vampires.

The medical officer's story appeared in newspapers all over Europe. Newspaper readers in cities like Paris and London went vampire crazy, and more newspapers published accounts of vampires being dug up in villages in remote eastern Europe.

By the end of the 1700s, the vampire craze had died down. Stories about actual vampires became very rare. Instead, vampires appeared more frequently in short stories and books.

Q: Why doesn't Dracula have any friends?

A: Because he's a pain in the neck.

Where in the World?

Find Romania on a map of the world. Put your finger on the toe of Italy's "boot" and move it diagonally up and to the right. Romania is located next to Russia. Now, look for Romania's neighbors, Hungary and Serbia. Those countries are where the vampire stories that we know came from.

WORDS to KNOW

decomposition: a natural process in which the body decays, or breaks down, after death. During *decomposition*, the skin changes color, the body swells, fluid leaks from the nose and mouth, and the fingernails and hair become loose. As a result, the hair and nails look as if they've grown.

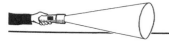
Real-Life Vampires?

Two people who actually lived in eastern Europe may have been the basis of vampire myths that spread throughout the area. One was Vlad Tepes (pronounced *se-pesh*), who was a prince of Romania from 1431 to 1476. His father was a very cruel king, and his subjects called him Dracul, which means "dragon" or "devil." Vlad Tepes was called Dracula, which means "son of Dracul."

Vlad Tepes's other nickname was Vlad the Impaler. He earned this nickname because he impaled thousands of his enemies on long stakes. After he died, legends about him spread throughout Europe. One story was that he had risen from his grave, like a vampire. His body was never found, so perhaps the story was true!

Another possible real-life vampire was Elizabeth Bathory, a countess who lived in Hungary from 1560 to 1614. Her nickname was the "Bloody Countess." She was obsessed with staying young and beautiful. She believed that blood would keep her from aging. So, she killed hundreds of young girls and took baths in their blood. She may even have drunk their blood! She was put on trial and then punished by being walled up in her bedroom for the rest of her life.

Neither Vlad Tepes nor Elizabeth Bathory was actually a *real* vampire, as far as we know. They were just very nasty rulers who murdered many of their subjects. The vampire legends that grew out of their evil deeds helped explain their cruelty by making them into monsters.

Dracula

The famous novel *Dracula* by Bram Stoker, published in 1897, was partly based on the legend of Vlad Tepes. In Stoker's

Ready to Read?

If you like vampires, you should read *Dracula*. Younger readers (grades two to four) will like the abridged Illustrated Eyewitness Classics version (DK Publishing, 1997). Older readers should try the complete version. Check the classics section of your local bookstore, or look for it in the library.

 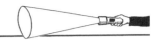
novel, Vlad Tepes, or Dracula, survived and lived for many centuries as a vampire in a castle in Transylvania. Transylvania is located in the mountains of Romania. Eventually, Dracula ran out of victims in the tiny village where he lived and decided to move to England. *Dracula* tells the story of how he came to England and how the first vampire hunters tried to kill him.

Dracula is most responsible for the way we think of vampires today. When you picture a vampire, you probably imagine a tall, thin man with jet-black hair, pale skin, red lips, and white fangs, wearing a long black cape— that was just how Stoker described Dracula. Before that book, vampires didn't wear capes, and they weren't very good-looking.

The book also introduced new "facts" about vampires. For example, *Dracula* taught us that vampires can't see their reflections in mirrors and that they can't enter a house unless they are invited.

Vampires Today

Today, vampires are more popular than ever. You can read about them in books, watch them in the movies and on TV, and even pretend to be a vampire when you're playing. Today's vampires are based on the myths of eastern Europe, on fictional stories like *Dracula*, and on vampire movies, which have been popular since the 1930s.

I Vant Your Vowels

This vampire knows that people think he is scary looking, not handsome. This makes him so cranky, he has sucked all the vowels out of the following words people use to describe monsters. See if you can put the vowels back in the proper words. HINT: Cross the letters off the list as you use them. Only the correct words will use up all the vowels!

1. CR __ __ P Y

2. FR __ G H T F __ L

3. GH __ S T L Y

4. GH __ __ L __ S H

5. SH __ C K __ N G

Modern vampires kept some of the characteristics of the ancient vampires, such as drinking blood and rising from the grave. But they have some new traits, too. A modern vampire might wear a cape or a tuxedo, while ancient vampires dressed in the robes or clothes they were buried in. Also, today's vampires can turn into bats and control animals; some can even fly. Vampires have come a long way!

Vampire Powers

Vampires have many supernatural powers. They can change into animals, such as bats, and they can command other animals, like wolves, to do things for them. Vampires have strange physical powers, too. They are strong enough to climb straight up walls, but they can also turn themselves into mist, which lets them squeeze underneath doors or around windows.

Vampires can see in the dark, and they have very good hearing. They can hear the beating of a human heart through walls and even many miles away. Vampires also have hypnotic eyes that put their victims in a trance. Once people are in a dreamy state, they're easier to bite.

The vampire's greatest power is living after death— being **undead**. Although vampires are technically dead, they drink blood from living creatures to keep their bodies from rotting. Blood also keeps vampires looking young and beautiful. Vampires don't have to drink human blood, although that is their favorite kind. They can drink animal blood, or they can just go down to the blood bank and make a withdrawal.

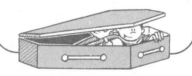

Bad Blood

Blood is extremely fattening. One liter of blood contains about 1,000 calories of high-fat, high-protein nutrition. So, even if drinking blood keeps you looking young, it won't keep you looking thin!

undead: a dead body that has been brought back to life, or reanimated, by a supernatural force. *Zombies* are also *undead* creatures. You'll learn more about them in Chapter 5.

Becoming a Vampire

The surest way to become a vampire is to be bitten by one. Usually, the vampire enters its victim's bedroom while the person is sleeping. If the person wakes up, the vampire can hypnotize him with its eyes and then bite his neck with its long fangs. Afterward, the vampire seals the wound so that it looks like two faint red marks. Just because a vampire bites you doesn't mean that you'll become one yourself. You can cure yourself by washing the bite with **holy water,** but it will probably sting—a lot!

Once a vampire chooses a victim, it returns night after night. During this time, the vampire's victim becomes weak, pale, and irritable. The victim stops eating and loses weight. Other signs that a vampire is visiting someone are sleeplessness, sleep-walking, and frequent nightmares. The victim avoids sunlight and garlic. Eventually, the person dies. Then he or she is sure to rise from the grave as a vampire.

Vampire legends describe many ways to keep new vampires from rising from their graves. You can drive stakes through the coffin lid or place a cross inside the coffin. You can bury new vampires upside down, so when they try to get out, they dig down into the earth instead of up to the surface. You can also tie up the new vampire with a rope containing many knots. Vampires are obsessed with untying knots, so getting free keeps them busy all night.

Being attacked by a vampire isn't the only way to become one, though. People once believed that babies born with a **caul,** teeth, a red birthmark, or a tail would probably become vampires. If a person lived an evil life, died violently, or committed suicide, he or she would turn into a vampire, as well. Someone

Q: Why did everyone call the vampire crazy?

A: They heard that he'd gone batty.

FUN FACT

Seedy Safety

What should you do if a vampire is chasing you? Throw a handful of seeds on the ground. The vampire must immediately stop to pick up and count every seed. That will keep it busy while you get away.

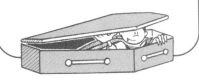

could even change into a vampire after death, if an animal like
a cat jumped over the coffin before the person was buried.

Fighting Vampires

Fighting vampires is serious business. Only hunt vampires
during the day, when they are asleep. At night, their powers
are greatest; during the day, they are much easier to kill.

First, assemble a vampire-hunting kit. Vampire hunters
should carry the following items with them at all times:

- A cross
- Holy water
- Lots of garlic
- A shovel for digging up graves
- Stakes made from ash, juniper, or blackthorn wood

Now that you're armed and ready, you can go looking for a
vampire. The best place to start is a graveyard where you think
a vampire might be sleeping. Take some vampire-hunter
friends with you—there's safety in numbers!

Why do vampires
go to art school?

Because they want
to draw blood!

Everything Kids'

http://www.everything.com

Why not throw a vampire theme party for Halloween this year? You'll
find lots of great decorating and costume ideas, recipes, and other
suggestions at *www.vamphalloween.com*.

Vampire Diseases

No one knows how the vampire legend got started. Most likely, these myths were told in part to explain mysterious diseases. Hundreds of years ago, people didn't understand medicine very well, so they invented stories to account for what they couldn't explain.

Catalepsy is a disorder of the nervous system that makes a person fall into a state of suspended animation. The breathing and heartbeat slow down; the muscles become rigid; and the victim can't move. People who have catalepsy look like they have died. Today, doctors can tell that the person is still alive, but long ago, people didn't know any better. Often, they buried victims of catalepsy while they were still alive. When the person woke from the coma, he or she tried to dig out of the grave. This may explain why vampires are the "living dead" who rise from their graves after they are buried.

Anemia is another disease that people didn't understand hundreds of years ago. People with anemia have an unusually low number of red blood cells. These cells carry oxygen throughout the body. So, people who have anemia don't get enough oxygen to their cells. Symptoms are a pale complexion, exhaustion, fainting, and loss of appetite. Before people knew about anemia, they may have thought that a person who had the disease was the victim of a vampire.

Today, vampires aren't as scary as they used to be. Some people like vampires so much that they try to be like them (although they don't drink blood or kill people). They dress up in fancy clothes and go out only at night. They even wear specially made fangs. There are over twenty-five active vampire interest groups in the United States and England. As you can see, our interest in vampires is as strong as ever.

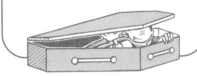

Bat Myth?

The vampire bat of Central and South America is not actually a vampire. A scientist named the bat after the vampire because of its habit of biting animals (like chickens, horses, and cows) and then licking their blood. The bat only drinks a few ounces of blood at a time, so it never kills the animals it bites. The vampire bat rarely attacks humans.

anemia: from a Greek word meaning "without blood." *Anemia* can be caused by a disease or by poor diet. People with the most common form of *anemia* usually get better by eating foods that contain a lot of iron, like spinach.

Make a
Vampire Costume

1. Use hair gel to slick back your hair or tease it into a wild hairdo. Vampires like to look glamorous! If you want to, you can spray a streak of white in your hair with temporary hair color.

2. Powder your face to make it look dead white, and paint your lips red, white, or black. Use eye shadow to put dark shadows under your eyes and darken the lids. Rimming your eyes with red or pink lip-liner also creates an effective dead look. (Get someone to help you with this part.)

3. Make fake blood by mixing one part corn syrup with two parts water and adding a few drops of red food coloring. If the blood looks too bright, add one or two drops of green food coloring. Put a few drops of blood at the corner of your mouth or on your chin. (The blood is edible, but the food coloring may stain your skin or clothes.)

4. Get dressed. Go traditional with a black cape and suit for the guys and a long, white dress for the girls. Or be a modern vampire who wears black clothes and a leather jacket. Colonial or medieval costumes work well, too. Use your imagination to create a vampire look that's all your own. Don't forget your fangs!

CHAPTER 2

WEREWOLVES AND OTHER SHAPESHIFTERS

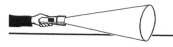 

What Is Shapeshifting?

A shapeshifter is a person who can change into an animal. This power is also called **lycanthropy**. Stories have been told about shapeshifters all over the world. Even the cave dwellers 20,000 years ago painted pictures of people changing into animals. Most cultures—including European, African, Indian, Japanese, and Native American cultures—have legends about people who can turn into animals.

The First Shapeshifters

Ancient people worshiped animals, especially the most ferocious hunters. They recognized that animals had talents that people did not. When hunting, people tried to become like the animals they revered, going on all fours and even wearing animal skins. They believed that if they actually became the animals, they would be more powerful hunters.

Priests of Native American and African tribes called **shamans** were able to change themselves into animals at will. Shamans could control the spirit world and become the animals that represented them, their totem animals, by using magic spells. Shamans often wore the skins of animals during their ritual dances to symbolize their totems.

In those early days, shapeshifters were great magicians and hunters. But as legends were told about them over the years, shapeshifters became monsters. The powers they got from changing into animals made them fierce and dangerous. They lost their human emotions and in animal form were able to commit crimes without feeling guilty.

Q: Who are the werewolf's cousins?

A: Whatwolf and whenwolf.

Kinds of Shapeshifters

All the legends about shapeshifters are very similar. The shapeshifter changes into an animal at sunset and then spends the night attacking and eating other people or animals. At dawn, the shapeshifter changes back to human form.

Shapeshifters can change into many different kinds of animals, depending on where they live. In Europe and America, where there are lots of wolves, shapeshifters typically change into werewolves. In Africa, shapeshifters may become were-lions or were-leopards. Ancient people in Mexico and Peru believed in were-jaguars, were-eagles, and were-serpents. Egypt had the greatest number of shapeshifters, where stories were told about were-tigers, were-elephants, were-crocodiles, and even were-sharks.

Werewolves: The Most Famous Shapeshifters

Of all the different kinds of shapeshifters, or **were-beasts,** werewolves are the best known. Werewolves are people who change into wolves when the moon is full.

Why Wolves?

Shapeshifters usually change into the most ferocious, dangerous animals around. For thousands of years, people in Europe and in many other parts of the world were most afraid of wolves. They believed that wolves were creatures of evil. Wolves were seen as cunning, swift, and cruel, and everyone knew they had very big appetites. People hunted wolves for these reasons, which is why so many kinds of wolves are endangered today.

Legendary Lobisòn

In Brazil and Argentina, the seventh son is always a shape-shifter called a *lobisòn.* In the legends, the *lobisòn* turns into a hairy creature, wanders through the mountains, and eats any dead animals he finds. He also attacks any people he comes across, and if they survive, they become *lobisòn,* too.

were-beasts: Creatures that are half-man, half-animal. The term *were-beasts* means "man-beasts." *Were* is an Old English word for "man." If you put the prefix *were-* in front of any animal's name, that means the animal is half-man. Can you imagine a were-turtle or a were-rabbit?

Now we know that wolves aren't evil. Wolves are intelligent hunters that travel in packs so they can better attack and kill their prey. If they can't get enough food, they sometimes kill livestock. Although they usually avoid humans, wolves that are sick with rabies or starving might attack a person.

When stories about shapeshifters spread to Europe, the most feared shapeshifter of all was the one who could turn himself into a wolf. For this reason, stories about werewolves were told more than stories about any other kind of shapeshifter.

Q: What happened to the werewolf who ate garlic?

A: His bark was worse than his bite.

Words to Know

metamorphosis: The complete change of physical form, such as from a human being into a wolf. *Metamorphosis* is usually accomplished by magic or other supernatural means.

The First Werewolf

In the earliest werewolf stories, werewolves didn't physically change into wolves. They just lost control of themselves and behaved violently, committing crimes without caring about what they did or who they hurt. They acted without conscience and were compared to wolves. They even symbolically became wolves by putting on wolf skins or costumes.

Ready to Read?

To learn more about Zeus and the other Greek gods, read the Greek myths for yourself. A good book to start with is *D'Aulaires' Book of Greek Myths* by Ingri D'Aulaire and Edgar Parin D'Aulaire (Picture Yearling, 1992), available in your library or at the bookstore.

Everything Kids'

http://www.everything.com

Over the years, people have hunted wolves almost to extinction. Today, many groups are trying to protect wolves and reintroduce them to the wild, including the North American Wolf Association (*www.nawa.org*) and the International Wolf Center (*www.wolf.org*). In the United States, wolves are making a big comeback.

As the stories changed over the years, the idea of **metamorphosis,** or someone physically changing from a person to a wolf, was introduced. The first person to actually change into a wolf that we know of was Lycaos, who appears in a Greek myth. Lycaos was a king in ancient Greece who grew proud and lazy over the years. The god Zeus visited Lycaos to check up on him. Lycaos showered the god with gifts and even offered to prepare an elaborate feast with his youngest son as the main course. Zeus was so angry that he punished Lycaos by turning him into a wolf.

The Werewolf Trials

In the sixteenth and seventeenth centuries in Europe, lots of people believed in werewolves. So many stories about werewolves were going around that it created a kind of hysteria. People accused of being werewolves were arrested and put on trial, and anyone convicted of being a werewolf was put to death. Between 1520 and 1630, there were over 32,000 werewolf trials in France alone!

The most famous werewolf trial happened in 1589 in Germany. A large wolf was terrorizing the countryside, attacking both people and animals. Peter Stubb was arrested and placed on trial for being a werewolf. After being tortured, he confessed to practicing black magic. He said that the devil had given him a magic belt that enabled him to turn into

By the Light of the Moon

Use the decoder to figure out the answer to this riddle:
What do you call a bad dream in which a werewolf is attacking you?

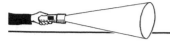 
a wolf. For that crime, he was sentenced to death. And no one ever found the magic belt . . .

The charge of being a werewolf disappeared from the European courts in the seventeenth century. People didn't stop believing in them, though. Even today, many people still think werewolves exist. Some people actually believe that they are werewolves themselves!

Werewolves among Us

If there are several nighttime animal attacks nearby, people may suspect that a werewolf is living among them. But unless they can catch the werewolf in the act, it's difficult to spot one.

Identifying Werewolves

Werewolves look different even when they are in human form. They usually have more hair than most people, especially on the palms of their hands. They have especially long third fingers and red-tinged fingernails. Werewolves' ears are pointy and set far back and low on the head. Their mouths and eyes are usually dry, and they are often thirsty. And of course, they have long, pointy teeth!

Werewolves also act differently than other people. They are often tired during the day because they have been running around all night. Werewolves may not eat much because they usually get their fill when they go out hunting. They also have many cuts and scratches from running around in the woods. Werewolves tend to be very sad and keep to themselves a lot.

One sure way to identify a werewolf is to hurt him while he is in wolf form. The wound remains when he changes back to

Q: Why did the werewolf have a stomachache?

A: It must have been someone he ate.

Where in the World?

Try to find France and Germany on a map. First, locate the continent of Europe. France is the large country on the west coast. Germany, another large country, is just east of France. These countries are where most werewolf legends started.

Mexican Mystery

There is a very rare genetic disease in which the entire body, particularly the face, is covered with hair. The medical name for this condition is hypertrichosis, but it is often called Werewolf Syndrome because the person with the disease looks like a wolfman. Little boys who had this disease used to be exhibited in circuses as "dog-faced boys." Today, the disease is so rare that it only appears in one family in Mexico.

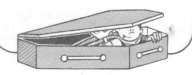

Everything Kids'

http://www.everything.com

Try out a fun game at *www.tcfhe.com/goosebumps/scairy.html*—it lets you make your own werewolf! You will need a software program called Shockwave; it's free if you go to *www.macromedia.com/ shockwave.*

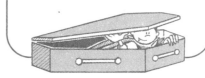

FUN FACT

Big Mouth!

Even in human form, werewolves have to sleep with their mouths wide open because it is very difficult for them to unclench their jaws. Wolf jaws are very strong so they can bite through the bones of their prey. The biting capacity of a wolf is 1,500 pounds of pressure per square inch. Compared to that, people are puny; we have a biting capacity of 300 pounds per square inch.

human form. To find the werewolf, locate the person with a suspicious cut in the same place where the wolf was hurt.

Becoming a Werewolf

There are so many ways to become a werewolf that it's amazing there aren't more of them. A person can become a werewolf on purpose or by accident.

Becoming a werewolf on purpose usually involves magic. The person must cast a spell and perform a special ritual. The ritual might involve drinking a special potion or rubbing a salve, or ointment, all over to make the change happen. The werewolf-to-be might also need to wear a belt or girdle made from wolf skin.

Anyone who wants to become a werewolf on purpose probably isn't a very nice person. In fact, witches and wizards who change themselves into werewolves are usually downright evil. They want to become werewolves so they can commit crimes at night with little fear of being hurt or caught. During the werewolf trials, most werewolves were thought to be evil sorcerers.

> Even a man wh~ ~ pure in heart and says his prayers by night, may become a wolf when the wolfbane blooms and the autumn moon is bright.

—From the movie
The Wolf Man
(Universal Studios, 1941)

The Navajo also tell legends about evil people in the tribe who changed into werewolves to steal, rob graves, and bring sickness.

It is much easier to become a werewolf by accident. Being bitten by another werewolf is a sure way to become one. Or, an evil magician can cast a spell on you or curse you so you change into a werewolf. Or, you might drink from a pool where wolves have drunk or sip water from the footprint of a wolf. (So don't go sipping water out of footprints!) Eating the meat or brains of a wolf can

Ho-Ho-Howl

The letters in each column go in the squares directly below them, but not in the same order! Black squares are the spaces between words. When you have correctly filled in the grid, you will have the answer to this riddle:

What is the difference between werewolves and kids at Christmas?

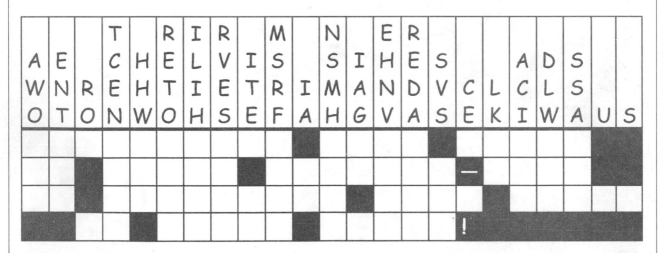

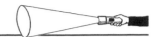

WORDS to KNOW

lunacy: absence of normal or usual thought or actions. The full moon has long been thought to make people act stranger than usual, and what could be crazier than changing into a wolf and running around all night attacking people? *Lunacy* comes from the Latin word *luna* for moon.

change you into a werewolf. Even being born on Christmas Eve can be enough to make you a werewolf. So can sleeping outside under the full moon, especially on a summer night. The full moon supposedly brings out strange behavior, or **lunacy.** Just ask a police officer, or a doctor or nurse who works in an emergency room!

Lycanthropy can also run in families. If the father or mother is a werewolf, the children will probably inherit that power.

When you read books or watch movies about werewolves today, they're likely to be about werewolves who became that way by accident. Usually, these werewolves don't want to change into wolves or attack people; they can't help it. Often they don't even remember what they did while they were in wolf form. Sometimes modern werewolves try to lock themselves up during the full moon so they won't commit any crimes. These werewolves are usually very sad and lonely; it's not their fault that they are monsters.

FUN FACT

Peculiar Potion

Becoming a werewolf on purpose usually involves magic. The person might have to drink a special potion or rub a salve, or ointment, all over to make the change happen. The werewolf-to-be might also need to wear a belt or girdle made from wolf skin.

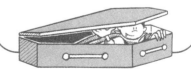

Observe the Moon's Phases

As you know, werewolves change when the moon is full. The moon has four phases: new, first quarter, full, and last quarter. At any time, the sun lights half of the moon, and the other half is dark. As the moon orbits the earth, we can see different portions of the lighted half (see the diagram). It takes the moon approximately twenty-eight days to orbit the earth, so it takes about seven days to move through each of the four phases.

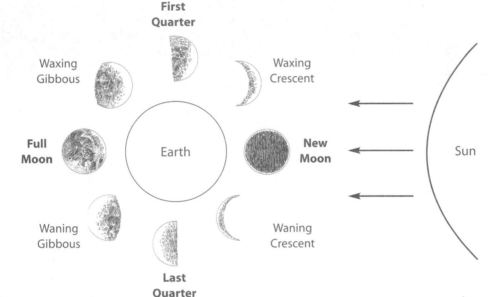

The four phases are in bold type in this example. Waxing and waning are the stages between each phase of the moon.

Make a calendar to find out exactly when the full moon is.

1. Get a calendar or make your own showing the next twenty-eight days.
2. Each night, go outside and look at the moon. Draw a picture of what it looks like in the day's box on your calendar.
3. Compare your drawing to the pictures in the diagram. Identify the correct moon phase and write its name in the box for that day on your calendar.
4. When the moon is full, draw a red circle around that day on your calendar. How many days, total, is the moon full each month? Beware, because the werewolves may be out during that time!

CHAPTER 3

GHOSTS AND OTHER THINGS THAT GO BUMP IN THE NIGHT

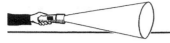

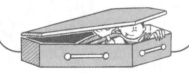

How does a flabby ghost slim down?

He rides an exorcise bike!

Spirits Who Stay Behind

Ghosts are the spirits of people who have died. These spirits are stuck in the world of the living, usually because they have unfinished business or because they experienced some great tragedy during their lives.

Many ghosts are invisible. When they do take on a form, they look like a hazy mist, a floating ball of light, or a transparent person wearing the clothing of their time. Ghosts can pass through doors and walls, and they can appear and disappear abruptly. Ghosts aren't usually dangerous, although seeing one could be very frightening.

Ghosts Around the World

Many people believe in ghosts, and stories about them are told in almost all countries. Some cultures have developed rituals to help spirits rest such as offering them food or clothing.

Belief in ghosts can be traced back more than 2,000 years. The ancient Greeks told the first ghost stories that we know about. The Greek philosopher Plato wrote about "the soul which survives the body" haunting the tombs of the dead. One of the earliest recorded ghost stories is about a Greek army commander who starved to death in the temple of the goddess Athena. The noises caused by his ghost terrified the worshipers. Finally, a sorcerer had to get rid of the spirit.

Types of Ghosts

When most people think of ghosts, they imagine a spirit who hangs around a place, like a haunted house, for a long time after its death. But there are many other types of ghosts, too.

Sometimes, a ghost appears just once, at the time of death, to someone many miles away. This appearance is the most commonly reported kind of ghost. It has a special name—crisis apparition—because it appears to a loved one at a time of great crisis. Usually, this type of ghost appears to say good-bye or to give a special message.

Ghosts aren't always people, either. Ghostly cars, motorcycles, trains, and ships have been seen, usually near the location of some tragic accident. Pets and other animals can also become ghosts.

Ghostly Theories

Some people don't think ghosts are the spirits of dead people at all. There are many theories to explain what ghosts actually are. Sometimes the theories are based on naturally occurring events like the **will-o'-the-wisp.**

One theory is that ghosts are the energy left behind by strong emotions or events. This theory could explain why ghosts are usually connected with great tragedies, such as murders, train crashes, and shipwrecks. Battlefields are often full of ghosts, too.

Others believe that ghosts are a result of **psychic** powers. People who are psychic pick up on strong images in a haunted place. They might see a person as he or she appeared many years ago and mistake that person for a ghost.

Q: What kind of street does a ghost like best?

A: A dead end.

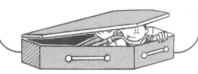

FUN FACT

English Hound

One kind of ghost that appears only in England is the Black Dog. This ghost looks like a large black dog with glowing eyes. It appears near roads, bridges, and cemeteries. Some stories say that Black Dogs appear to foretell the death of a loved one. Others say that Black Dogs protect travelers from harm or lead them to safety when they're lost.

WORDS to KNOW

will o' the wisp: a natural phenomenon, also called corpse candles, foxfire, and elf light. When pockets of swamp gas light up, they form glowing blue balls of light that can look like ghosts.

Some ghosts can be seen performing the same actions again and again. These ghosts don't usually notice if anyone is watching. Some people believe that these sightings might occur at "thin" places where you can actually see backward in time and watch an event that happened years or even centuries ago. Ghosts who repeat past actions are called atmospheric apparitions.

Of course it is possible that ghosts are just figments of our imagination. What do you think?

Tracking Down Ghosts

Ghosts have always fascinated people. A lot of people would like to see a ghost or talk to one. Over the years, people who want to see or meet ghosts have developed ways to gather evidence that ghosts exist, find them, and communicate with them.

FUN FACT

Possessed Possessions

Even objects can be haunted by people who once owned them. The objects may move when no one is touching them, and strange occurrences, like mysterious lights and sounds, may happen nearby. Common haunted objects include jewelry, collectibles, clocks, furniture, and paintings.

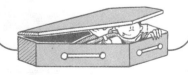

Haunted Places

Usually, each ghost hangs around, or haunts, one place, such as a house or a graveyard. A place with a ghost in it is said to be haunted. Ghosts generally **haunt** the places where they died, although they might also hang around houses where they lived or other places that were important to them.

Q: What do you call a ghost's mother and father?

A: Trans-parents.

The most popular places for ghosts to haunt are houses—not just old mansions and castles, but also modern houses. (You may even live in a haunted house!) But ghosts can be found almost anywhere: hotels, theaters, office buildings, stores, courthouses, prisons, churches, schools, colleges, railroad tracks, bridges, and cemeteries.

Haunted houses can be scary (and exciting) places to live. Ghosts can make doors open and close by themselves, turn lights on and off, and move objects around. Rooms may get cold for no reason. Ghosts often make strange noises during the night, too. Spooky sounds like thumps, creaks, whispers, and sobs can all be from ghosts. Phantom footsteps may be heard in the hall or on the stairs, or ghostly music might come from nowhere. Strange lights may move past darkened windows. People who live in the house may feel as though someone is touching them or is in the room with them, even when no one is there.

WORDS to KNOW

haunt: from the same root as the word *home.* So, the place a ghost *haunts* is actually its home. In some areas, *haunt* is also another word for ghost.

Famous Hauntings

There are thousands of haunted places all around the world. Many of these places are open to the public, so you can visit them and try to spot a ghost. Find a list of haunted places to visit at *www.haunted-places.com.*

The Tower of London is one of England's most haunted places. Many executions, tortures, and poisonings took place there, which is probably why so many ghosts haunt it. The

Ready to Read?

You can find many books of ghost stories in your local library. Two favorites about ghosts in the United States are *Haunted America* and *Historic Haunted America,* both written by Michael Norman and Beth Scott (Tor, 1999).

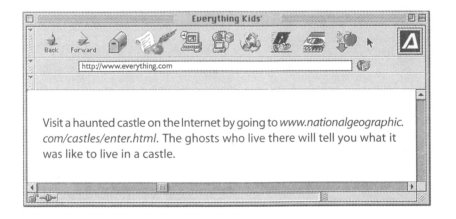

Everything Kids'

http://www.everything.com

Visit a haunted castle on the Internet by going to *www.nationalgeographic. com/castles/enter.html.* The ghosts who live there will tell you what it was like to live in a castle.

Boo Who?

These haunted rooms are full of ghostly faces. Which three faces do not appear in both rooms?

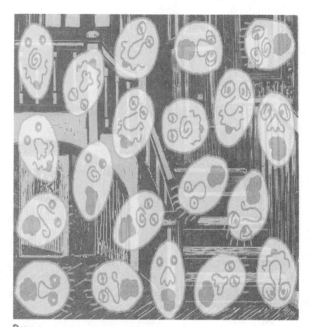

Room 1

Room 2

most famous ghost at the Tower is Anne Boleyn, one of the eight wives of King Henry VIII. The king had her beheaded so he could marry someone else. Now, she can be seen walking around the Tower, carrying her head under her arm.

The Whaley House in San Diego, California, is a famous haunted house. In fact, the U.S. Department of Commerce has designated it as officially haunted. It was first opened to the public in 1960. Since then,

many visitors have observed the ghost's activities, including ghostly visions, cold spots, a feeling of being touched or watched when no one is there, unexplainable lights, phantom footsteps and tappings, objects moving by themselves, and odd smells.

Another famous haunted house is the Winchester Mystery House in San Jose, California. Sarah Winchester inherited a fortune from her family business, which made Winchester rifles. She believed that the spirits of

everyone killed by the rifles placed a curse on her family. To appease the spirits, Mrs. Winchester decided to start building a mansion and keep building it forever. The mansion was constructed for thirty-eight years, until her death. Over 600 rooms were added, with odd features like doors that opened onto empty space, windows on inside walls, and secret passages. Now, her ghost haunts the house and has been seen many times.

Alcatraz, the island prison in San Francisco, California, has a large number of ghosts. The prison was closed in 1963 and was later opened to tourists. Since then, visitors have heard unexplainable crashing sounds and screams. Visitors have reported seeing cell doors close by themselves and feeling as if they were being watched. The most haunted areas of the prison are the warden's house, the hospital, the laundry room, and Cellblock C, where three convicts died during an escape attempt.

Another famous haunted place is the Alamo in San Antonio, Texas. The Alamo is a famous landmark of Texas history. In 1836, 4,000 Mexican troops attacked it. The eleven-day battle killed most of the fortress's defenders. Since then, people have seen ghostly hands coming out of the walls of the fortress and a ghost walking back and forth on top of the wall.

Ghost Hunting

Some people belong to clubs that hunt ghosts. These clubs find haunted houses and other haunted places and try to gather evidence that the ghosts really exist. They take pictures and videos of the ghosts and record the noises they make.

One tool that ghost hunters use is called an Electro-Magnetic Field Detector, or EMF for short. Ghost hunters believe that when a ghost appears, it disturbs the magnetic field. The EMF can detect these disturbances and let the ghost hunters know if a ghost is around.

FUN FACT

Haunted House

The most famous ghost in the United States is President Abraham Lincoln, who has been seen walking through the halls of the White House, in the Oval Office, and in his old bedroom. Lincoln's ghost has also been spotted near his grave in Springfield, Illinois, and some people have seen the ghost of his funeral train.

Where in the World?

Find the famous Alamo on a map. First, locate the state of Texas. San Antonio is in the southern part of the state, close to the Mexican border. Perhaps you might want to visit the Alamo with your family and look for ghosts!

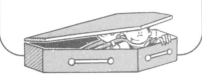

Contacting Ghosts

People have always tried to contact the dead and talk to them. In ancient times, shamans and sorcerers could talk with the dead and pass messages to their loved ones.

During the late 1800s, Spiritualism became very popular in the United States and Europe. People who practice Spiritualism use a ritual called a séance to get in touch with ghosts. The séance is led by a medium, a person who has the ability to contact the "other side." Everyone participating sits around a table and holds hands while the medium contacts the spirits. The ghosts communicate by rapping on the table, using the medium to write messages, or talking in their own voices through the medium's mouth. Sometimes the table floats through the air, or **ectoplasm** appears.

Spiritualism started in 1848 in New York State. The Fox family believed that they had a ghost in their house. They could hear phantom footsteps and what sounded like someone knocking on the walls. Two of the children, Margaretta (who was fourteen years old) and Kate (who was twelve years old), began to talk to the ghost. They developed a system of raps through which the ghost could give them messages. The girls became very famous mediums, holding séances all over the United States and in Europe.

Many mediums were shown to be frauds, though. They faked the ghost's appearances using tricks like hidden wires and masks covered with sheets. Nevertheless, people still believe in mediums. They even appear on television talk shows.

WORDS to KNOW

ectoplasm: a slimy residue that ghosts leave behind. Mediums who are talking to ghosts may have *ectoplasm* flow out of their noses and mouths.

Q: What did one ghost say to the other ghost?

A: "I don't believe in people."

Another way to contact ghosts is to use an Ouija board. The Ouija board has all the letters and numbers printed on it, plus the words *yes*, *no*, and *good-bye*. It comes with a small wooden pointer. Several people gather around the board and put their fingertips on the pointer. The pointer moves to different letters and words to spell out the message that the ghost wants to give.

Putting Ghosts to Rest

Because most ghosts have unfinished business, the best way to get rid of them is to find out what they need to resolve. For instance, if the ghost was murdered, you could find out who killed the original person, and get justice.

Silly Séance

Connect the numbered dots, then connect the lettered dots to find out the answer to this riddle:

Why did the ghost use the computer?

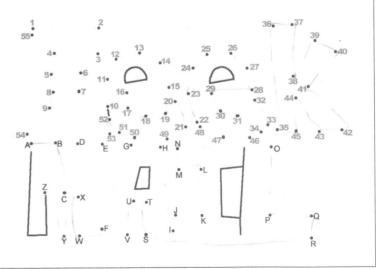

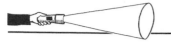 
> From ghoulies and ghosties,
> And long-leggedy beasties,
> And things that go bump in the night,
> Good Lord, deliver us!
>
> —Traditional Scottish prayer

I See a Ghost

Color in all the letters that are not in the word "BOO" to find the answer to this riddle:

What happens to actors when a ghost haunts the theater?

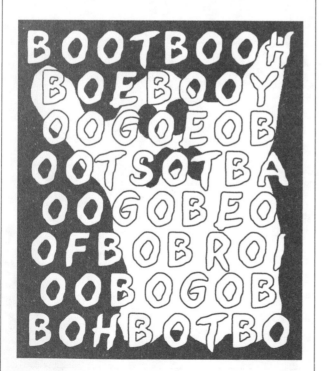

Sometimes, you can't find out what the ghost needs to rest in peace. In those cases, you can try other things. Prayer sometimes works, as does reburying the ghost's body properly. Some people perform exorcisms to get rid of ghosts. An exorcism is a ceremony, usually performed by a priest, to banish a spirit that is haunting a place or a person.

Other Ghostly Monsters

Other kinds of monsters act like ghosts by making strange noises, moving objects around, and haunting houses and graveyards, but they really aren't ghosts at all. These monsters include poltergeists and the bogeyman.

Patient: Doctor, Doctor, I keep thinking I'm a ghost!

Doctor: I thought that might be your problem when you came into my office through the wall!

Poltergeists

Poltergeists are a particularly annoying type of spirit. Unlike ghosts who haunt places, poltergeists haunt people. Even if the person moves to a new house, the poltergeist will follow. Poltergeists usually haunt teenagers, particularly teenagers who are under a lot of stress or are very unhappy.

Poltergeists are very destructive, and they always cause trouble. They move things around, throw objects, overturn furniture, break windows, set fires, make water drip down the walls, and cause stones to fall from the sky. They may also pull hair and slap and bite people. Although poltergeists don't usually hurt people, they can be dangerous if you get in the way of their activities.

Most ghost experts don't believe that poltergeists are ghosts at all. Rather, they think that poltergeists are a form of psychic energy that's out of control. The person who is haunted by the poltergeist is the one who's actually causing all the damage because of stress or strong emotions. Sometimes, the poltergeist disappears as suddenly as it showed up.

The Bogeyman

The **bogeyman** is a mischievous spirit that likes nothing better than playing practical jokes. For instance, it may pull the covers off the bed while someone is sleeping or hover just behind someone's back in an empty room. The bogeyman is more annoying than dangerous.

The bogeyman lives in dark places, such as cupboards, closets, cellars, and attics. Outdoors, he prefers barns, caves, and abandoned mines. At night, he comes out to move around the house, making bumps, scuffles, and creaks. He doesn't really look like anything, just a large puff of dust.

WORDS to KNOW

poltergeist: the German word for "noisy ghost." Of all the kinds of ghosts, *poltergeists* make the most noise and cause the most destruction.

bogeyman: any scary monster or person, or anything frightening that we don't know much about.

FUN FACT

Spiritual Ceremony

Tibetan priests have a ceremony called shedür for exorcising ghosts. The ceremony takes six days. First, the priest discovers the ghost's identity. Then, he creates a doll and he seals the ghost inside. He cuts the doll into pieces, burns it, and buries the ashes. This action releases the spirit so it can be reborn.

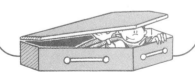

Play the Haunted House Game

At your next Halloween party or spooky gathering, play a ghostly game that will keep your guests guessing. You will need several small boxes, such as shoeboxes. Cut a hole in the top or front of each box just big enough to put a hand into. Put a different gross object inside each box. Have your guests stick their hands in the boxes and try to guess what's inside.

Here are some suggestions for things to put inside the boxes:

- Blood (Make fake blood using the recipe in Chapter 1, and put it in a bowl inside the box. Your guests will see the blood when they take their hands out of the box. You can also try this trick with glow-in-the-dark or red paint—just make sure it washes off!)
- Bones (chicken bones or fake bones)
- Brains (Jell-O)
- Eyeballs (peeled grapes or wet olives)
- Fingers (cut-up hot dogs)
- Guts (cold, wet spaghetti)
- Hair (a wig)
- Hand (Fill a latex glove with pudding.)
- Mice (a battery-powered mouse toy—leave it running for a real scare!)
- Spider webs (stretched cotton or wet string)
- Spiders (fake rubber spiders)
- Teeth (unpopped popcorn)

CHAPTER 4

THE GOBLINS WILL GET YOU IF YOU DON'T WATCH OUT

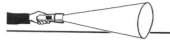

goblin: from the Greek word *kobalos,* which means "rogue." A rogue is a dishonest, worthless, or mischievous person. This is a good name for *goblins,* because they are villains who like nothing better than causing trouble.

❝ You better mind your
parents and your
teachers fond and dear . . .
Or the goblins will get ya if
ya don't watch out! ❞

—From the poem
"Little Orphan Annie"
by James Whitcomb Riley
(1849–1916)

Those Gruesome Goblins

Goblins can be found throughout Europe. Stories about goblins are told all over the continent, from Scandinavia to France and Germany, but most goblins live in Great Britain and Ireland. They prefer dark places, like under rocks and in the roots of trees. Goblins are hard to find, though, because they never stay in one place for very long.

Goblins look like small, ugly people. They are very short, often no more than three or four feet tall. They almost always have some kind of strange feature, such as pointed ears or webbed feet. Some goblins look like animals, and some are shapeshifters that can change into animals and objects.

Q: Why wasn't there any food left after the monster party?

A: Because everybody was a goblin'.

Fairies and Goblins

Goblins are actually a type of fairy. We usually think of fairies as beautiful creatures that bring good luck, such as hidden treasure. Goblins, on the other hand, are evil and malicious, and they always bring bad luck. They often come out on Halloween to play tricks.

Goblins are the ugly side of fairies. While some fairies are very helpful, goblins cause nothing but trouble. They are thieves who steal food, clothing, and valuable objects from people and even kidnap babies. They also take pleasure in spoiling luck, causing misfortune, and generally making life difficult.

Many goblins like to punish wicked people, especially criminals, liars, and those who are lazy and selfish. The best way to stay on a goblin's good side is to act polite, work hard, and always tell the truth.

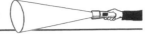

Everything Kids'

http://www.everything.com

Want to learn more about the wonderful world of fairies? Go to *http://thefae.freeservers.com* to meet different kinds of fairies and read fairy tales.

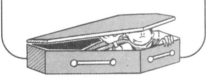

FUN FACT

Better Than Beets?

People once believed that monsters wandered around freely on Halloween. In Ireland, they carved beets and turnips into gruesome goblin faces to scare the real monsters away. When the Irish came to the United States, they found that pumpkins were more plentiful (and easier to carve), so they used them instead. That's how the tradition of carving jack-o'-lanterns started.

Goblins as Practical Jokers

Goblins love nothing more than to play practical jokes. They have the most fun when they annoy people and make them look like fools. Their jokes are usually just irritating, but sometimes they can be downright dangerous.

Some favorite goblin tricks include:

- Changing road signs
- Destroying crops
- Misleading travelers
- Pinching
- Pulling off the covers while people are sleeping
- Scaring people
- Spilling milk
- Stealing small objects
- Tangling hair
- Throwing and breaking things

WORDS to KNOW

bugbear or hobgoblin: two other names for *goblin. Bugbear* and *hobgoblin* also mean anything that is difficult, frustrating, or frightening. For instance, you might say, "My math homework is a real *bugbear.*"

Monsters and other creatures that like to play jokes are called tricksters. Tricksters can be found in the stories of cultures all over the world. Another trickster that you read

about in Chapter 3 is the bogeyman. Demons, devils, and **phookas** are also trickster monsters.

In other cultures, tricksters can be gods, animals, or shapeshifters. Although they come in many forms, tricksters share the same goal: to play practical jokes, particularly on people who are too serious or who follow the rules too strictly. Is it possible that all that tricksters are really trying to tell us is to lighten up and have some fun?

Changelings

A favorite trick of all goblins is to kidnap a human baby and leave a changeling in its crib. The changeling is a goblin baby that causes no end of trouble for the parents. It looks just like the kidnapped baby, except it may have some goblin feature, such as large pointed ears. The changeling baby has a big appetite and is just as malicious as any goblin.

If a baby is kidnapped by goblins, the family can get the baby back by playing a trick on the changeling. A good trick is to pretend to brew water in the empty halves of an eggshell. This amazes the changeling, who will talk, revealing its fairy nature. Then the goblin must fly up the chimney to get away. The goblins will bring the real baby home soon afterward.

> **Q:** What do goblins mail home while on vacation?
> **A:** Ghost-cards.

Types of Goblins

The family of goblins is very large. While each species of goblins looks and acts differently, they all share two basic characteristics: they are all ugly, and they all love to play practical jokes.

FUN FACT

Helpful Hints

Brownies are a little bit goblin *and* a little bit fairy. They are playful like goblins but really try to be helpful, too.

WORDS to KNOW

gremlin effect: the tendency for things to go wrong at the worst possible time due to unexplained glitches.

A Different History

No one has more stories about tricksters than the Native Americans. In their stories, the trickster is often an animal, such as a spider, fox, coyote, rabbit, or raven. If you'd like to read some Native American trickster stories, look for *American Indian Trickster Tales* by Richard Erdoes and Alfonso Ortiz (Penguin, 1999).

Gremlins

Gremlins are the youngest of the goblin family. They first appeared during World War I, but they didn't become well known until World War II.

Gremlins are goblins of the technological age. They are very good at working with tools and machinery. Once, gremlins helped people come up with new inventions. But they got mad when the human inventors took all the credit. To get revenge, they make machinery break down.

Gremlins cause all kinds of problems. If you hit your thumb with a hammer, blame it on a gremlin. You can also blame gremlins for broken tools, flat tires, and burned toast. They turn off alarm clocks without waking you up and make the hot water run out when you're taking a shower. Every household has its very own gremlin that lives in one of the appliances (the one that breaks the most).

phooka: a shapeshifting *goblin* that can appear as an animal like a dog, a bull, or an eagle. The *phooka's* favorite form is a jet-black horse with blazing eyes. It offers travelers a ride, taking them on a terrifying gallop across the countryside and then dumping them in the mud. (The *phooka* thinks this is very funny.)

Trolls

Trolls are gigantic goblins that live in the forests, mountains, moors, and underground caves of Germany and Scandinavia. They guard bridges and lonely roads, demanding payment from travelers who want to pass through their domain. Trolls are extremely ugly creatures that are covered with hair. They are very stupid and vulgar, and they hate both fairies and people equally.

Trolls come out most often during the "light nights" of the summer in the far north of Europe. When a troll is around, hens don't lay eggs, cows don't give milk, horses won't work, and dogs and cats hide. Sometimes, trolls attack people or kidnap sleeping children. More often, they just peep through windows and scare the people inside.

Trolls can only go out at night. If they are caught outside in direct sunlight, they turn into stone.

Knockers

Knockers are goblins that live in mines. Although they are mischievous and like to play pranks, they are the nicest of the goblins. They make knocking noises to show miners where rich veins of ore can be found or to warn them of a cave-in. The miners must leave food for the knockers, or the knockers get angry and cause bad luck.

Sometimes, knockers guard the treasure found inside mines. In those cases, it can be very dangerous to go down into the mine. If someone tries to lower down on a rope, a hand will appear with a knife and cut the rope, sending the person falling to the bottom of the mineshaft. In the morning, the body will be neatly laid out at the top of the shaft.

Bogies and Spriggans

Two of the most dangerous and the ugliest kinds of goblins are bogies and spriggans.

Bogies live in swampy, muddy areas called bogs, which is how they got their name. They have a very bad temper. They most often punish liars and murderers, but they are also known for leading travelers astray so they get lost in the swamp. Bogies have many other names, including bogles, ballybugs, and bug-a-boos.

Spriggans are the ugliest and wickedest of all the goblins. They usually live near old ruins and castles. Although spriggans are quite small, they can blow themselves up into monstrous forms. They use this talent to scare away anybody who comes near.

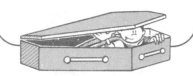

FUN FACT

No Night Lights!

In northern Europe, the sun never truly sets during the summer months, so it remains daylight or twilight twenty-four hours a day. The northern Europeans call the nights of summer "light nights." How do they get any sleep?

WORDS to KNOW

knockers: one of the largest species of goblins, *knockers* have many different names depending on where they live. In northern Germany, they are called *kobolds,* and in southern Germany, they are called *wichtlein.*

The spriggans' job is to guard buried treasure, and they will fight anyone who tries to take their riches from them. They are clever thieves and will rob houses to add to their treasure troves. They are also the worst of the baby-snatchers and take delight in kidnapping a human baby and leaving an ugly spriggan in its place.

Goblins: Where Bad Luck Comes From

Goblins are the **scapegoats** for the little annoyances of life, as well as for great tragedies like plane crashes, which can be blamed on gremlins, and mine cave-ins, which can be blamed on angry knockers. Goblins take the blame for everything from missing socks to flat tires and unexplained illness.

WORDS to KNOW

scapegoat: someone who takes the blame for mistakes or bad deeds committed by others. The term *scapegoat* comes from a biblical custom in which everyone's sins were symbolically placed on the head of a goat that carried the sins away into the wilderness.

Come Back Here!

All the G-O-B-L-I-N-S have run away from this list of goblin names, and rearranged the letters, too. What troublemakers! See if you can figure out which letters each name needs, and put the unscrambled names into the criss-cross grid.

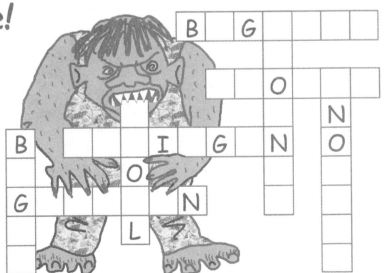

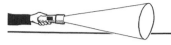

Bloody Bandit

One particularly evil goblin is called Red Cap. He lives in the ruined castles along the border between England and Scotland. He has large, fiery red eyes, long gray hair, and eagle's talons instead of hands. He always wears a red cap, which is dyed with the blood of his victims.

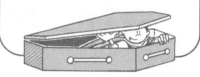

There are plenty of ways to protect yourself from meddling goblins. The Bible, a cross, prayers, running water, salt, and bells all keep goblins away. All fairies hate iron, so hanging an iron horseshoe over the front door will keep them from coming into the house. When walking alone at night, you can stop goblins from playing tricks on you by turning your clothes inside out or tying a piece of red thread to your clothes.

Instead of getting mad at the goblins, try to get on their good side. Before you go to bed, leave out a little bread and milk for them to snack on. Be nice to other people, too, and don't lie or steal. Your extra efforts to be good will please goblins because they particularly like to punish the wicked. You may just find your bad luck turning to good.

Q: Where did the goblin throw the football?

A: Over the ghoul line.

Where in the World?

Most fairy stories come from Great Britain, which is made up of the countries of England, Scotland, and Wales, and from the Republic of Ireland. On your map, locate Europe and put your finger on France. Move your finger north across the water—the English Channel. The big island is Great Britain, and the smaller island to the west is Ireland.

Make Goblin
Face Paint

Next Halloween, or maybe just for fun, paint your face to look like a goblin. This activity is a lot of fun to do with a friend. You can take turns giving each other the most gruesome faces. For each color, you'll need the supplies listed here.

Ingredients

1 teaspoon cornstarch
½ teaspoon cold cream
½ teaspoon water
Food coloring
Sponge

Directions

1. Mix the cornstarch, cold cream, and water.
2. Add one or two drops of food coloring to get the color you want.
3. Use a sponge to paint the makeup on each other's faces and create gruesome goblin faces—the uglier, the better.

You might find these hints helpful, too:

- Mix the paints in a muffin tin or custard cups so you can have several colors.
- Try mixing different colors together to make new colors.
- You can also stick wet oatmeal on your face, and then paint over it to make ugly lumps.

Be sure to keep the makeup away from your mouth and eyes (use lipstick and eye shadow instead).

CHAPTER 5
ZOMBIES: THE WALKING DEAD

WORDS to KNOW

reanimate: to bring a dead person or animal back to life, or make it appear alive again using magical or scientific means.

zombie: from the African word *mzombi*, which means "spirit of a dead person." *Zombie* can also refer to a person who acts like a robot or shows no emotion or energy. If you don't get enough sleep at night, you may be a *zombie* in the morning.

Voodoo or Vodou: from a West African word, *vodu*, which means "spirit" or "god." Most Haitians don't like the term *Voodoo*, though. They prefer their own name: Vodou.

FUN FACT

Banning Zombies

Many people in Haiti believe that zombies are real. Since 1835 there has been a Haitian law against making zombies. If a bokor is caught making a zombie, he has to pay a fine or even go to jail.

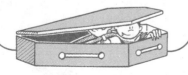

Called from the Grave

A zombie is a dead body that has no soul. Although the body can walk and get around, the person inside is still dead. The body has been **reanimated**. Like vampires, zombies are the undead; they are neither completely alive nor completely dead.

Unlike vampires, though, **zombies** don't look very good. Their bodies are dead and may even start to rot. Zombies can't move very well and are listless and clumsy. They have blank, staring eyes and a nasal voice. When they speak, they use few words and often repeat themselves. These characteristics make zombies stand out from ordinary people.

That Voodoo That You Do

Zombies are associated with the religion of **Voodoo**. The Voodoo religion developed in the country of Haiti. During colonial times, people from many different tribes in West Africa were kidnapped and brought to Haiti to work as slaves. Their masters didn't allow them to practice their tribal religions. The slaves kept their religions alive by worshiping in secret. The customs and beliefs of the different African tribes mingled to form a new religion. The slaves also brought in some of the beliefs of the native Indians and the Catholic customs of their masters. This new religion was called Voodoo.

Q: What did the friend say when the zombie introduced his girlfriend?

A: "Where did you dig her up?"

People who practice Voodoo believe in thousands of spirits called the lwa (pronounced "lo-a"), who give advice and help the living. People "serve" the lwa by honoring them with food, gifts, and rituals that involve dancing, drumming, and chanting.

When a respected person in the Voodoo community dies, his or her spirit also becomes a lwa.

Making a zombie depends on capturing the person's spirit. The spirit is very important to Voodoo beliefs. Without a spirit, a person has no free will. He can't make decisions for himself or do anything on his own.

Voodoo and Black Magic

The leaders of the Voodoo community are priests called houngans and priestesses are called mambos. Priests and priestesses of Voodoo practice white magic. They consider black magic to be evil. The houngans and mambos use Voodoo only for good purposes, such as curing disease, bringing good fortune, and solving problems.

A Voodoo priest who practices black magic is called a **bokor**. Once he starts doing black magic, he is no longer considered a real priest, and he is rejected by the Voodoo community. He always works in secret, selling his services for a high price.

Q: Why did the doctor tell the zombie to get some rest?

A: He was dead on his feet.

FUN FACT

Servant Spirits

Another kind of zombie in Voodoo is the zombie astral. This zombie is a spirit without a body. The black magician captures the spirit after death and puts it in a glass jar. The sorcerer can then command the spirit to perform tasks for him.

Where in the World?

Haiti is located on an island in the Caribbean Sea. Get a map and put your finger on the tip of Florida. Move your finger south until you find Cuba. Immediately east of Cuba is an island called Hispaniola. Haiti is located on the western third of the island.

WORDS to KNOW

bokor: a sorcerer who practices both white magic and black magic. In Voodoo, white magic is done with the right hand and black magic with the left hand. So, a *bokor* is said to be someone who serves the lwa "with both hands."

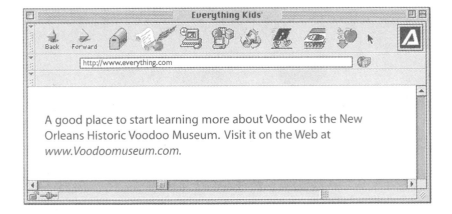

A good place to start learning more about Voodoo is the New Orleans Historic Voodoo Museum. Visit it on the Web at *www.Voodoomuseum.com.*

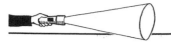 

zombify: to turn someone into a zombie. The entire process of changing someone into a zombie is called *zombification*.

Making a Zombie

One of the bokor's specialties is making a zombie. Bokors jealously guard the secret of making a zombie. They don't want just anybody to be able to make one!

When a bokor decides to make a zombie, he chooses a victim. He spreads a magic powder on the victim's threshold. When the victim walks across the powder, he absorbs the zombie powder through his feet. Or, the bokor might put the zombie powder in his victim's food. Shortly afterward, the person dies. After the funeral, the bokor goes to the grave and uses a magic spell to make the victim come to life as a zombie.

Once a bokor makes a zombie, he is the zombie's master. The zombie must obey the orders of the black magician who has his spirit. Being **zombified** is considered the supreme punishment in Haiti. That's because all of the people of Haiti used to be slaves. In the late 1700s, the slaves overthrew their masters and drove them out of the country. This was the only successful slave revolt in Western history. The worst thing a Haitian can imagine is being turned into a zombie, which means becoming a slave again.

Sometimes, the bokor will zombify a person who has made him angry. Some bokors form secret societies that punish bad people by making them zombies. Lazy people, slobs, and liars are in the most danger of being changed into zombies.

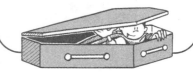

Duppy Prevention

In Jamaica and other islands in the West Indies, some people believe in a type of zombie called a duppy. A black magician can raise a duppy by going to its grave and calling its name over and over. The duppy can cause vomiting just by breathing on a person or cause convulsions just by touching a person's skin. Sprinkling tobacco seeds around the house keeps the duppy away.

The Zombie Powder

The recipe for the zombie powder is a closely guarded secret, and no one knows exactly what's in it. The ingredients are substances from many plants and animals, including poisonous ones. Zombie powder might contain millipedes, tarantulas, the skins of poisonous tree frogs, or seeds and leaves from poisonous plants.

One of the ingredients of the zombie powder is the puffer fish, which contains tetrodotoxin, one of the most poisonous substances in the world. This poison is so powerful that it can be absorbed through the skin; just a little bit is fatal. More than half the victims of puffer fish poisoning die within a short time. There is no known antidote for the poison.

Zombie Cures and Prevention

It doesn't take much to get rid of a zombie. All you have to do is give it some salt. Just the taste of salt is enough to remind the zombie what it's like to be alive. The zombie realizes that it has become undead and will no longer obey its master. The zombie is then free to return to its grave.

Natural Causes

Many Haitians believe in **zombies**, but few have ever seen one. There are some recorded instances of people who have claimed to see zombies, but there is no convincing evidence that zombies are real.

Some people who have studied Voodoo don't believe that zombies exist. They think that zombies are actually living people who were mistaken for zombies because of severe medical problems. Conditions like **schizophrenia** or mental disabilities can make people seem like zombies.

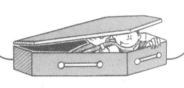

FUN FACT

Pricey Puffers

The puffer fish is a delicacy of Japanese sushi. A licensed chef must prepare it in a special way. Even so, it is still very dangerous to eat. It's also very expensive; one piece of fish can cost more than $200!

WORDS to KNOW

schizophrenia: a disease of the brain. *Schizophrenia* often makes a person withdraw from reality. A person with *schizophrenia* may move slowly or clumsily, may not respond to others, and may not have any interest in life. All of these symptoms can be mistaken for the characteristics of a zombie.

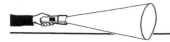

British scientists studied three Haitians who were supposed to be zombies. All three people were alive but had diseases that produced zombie-like symptoms. The scientists concluded that most zombies were actually living people who were just mistaken for zombies because their diseases weren't understood very well in Haiti.

Hollywood Zombies

Voodoo is a mysterious religion, and most people don't know a lot about it. For much of its history, Haiti was an isolated place with few visitors from other countries. People who did visit, however, came home with fascinating stories about Voodoo magic, secret rituals, and zombies. Although most of the stories were

Crossing Guard

Cross off the words from the following list according to the instructions. Then read the remaining words, but from right to left, and bottom to top. You will find the answer to this ancient riddle: Why did the zombie cross the road?

Cross out:
2 synonyms for "freezing"
2 antonyms for "right"
4 words meaning "old"
4 "odd numbers"
4 words that mean "strange"
5 "jobs"
4 "kinds of shoes"

doctor frigid boots to nine
icy him wrong eleven clogs
baker told vintage bokor three
incorrect bizarre senior dancer
teacher the sandals aged
seven weird sneakers cook
peculiar odd because antique

 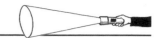
untrue or exaggerated, they caught the imagination of the public and of Hollywood. Zombies quickly became a favorite monster for the movies.

The zombies you see in movies don't bear much resemblance to the zombies of Voodoo folklore. For one thing, Voodoo zombies aren't really dangerous. They don't attack people or try to eat them. People who practice Voodoo are much more afraid of being changed into a zombie than they are of meeting one.

Movie zombies are much scarier than real ones. They usually have only one thing on their minds: eating people, particularly their brains. Because zombies move so slowly, they are easy to get away from, but they are very persistent. If there are too many around, watch out!

Why are movie zombies so fond of eating brains? Supposedly, to keep moving, they require a chemical found in the brain. Without this chemical, their bodies stop working, and eventually they lie down and become dead again.

Movie zombies come to life in ways other than black magic. In some movies, a toxic chemical spill turns all the dead bodies nearby into zombies. In other movies, mad scientists reanimate the dead as weird science experiments. Or aliens invading earth release a virus into the air that raises the dead so they can be used as an army against the living.

Who knows if zombies are real? One thing is sure: they will live on in movies and books for a long time.

Q: What kind of clothes do zombies wear?

A: Decay NY.

Ready to Read?

Have you ever wondered how they make monsters in the movies look so scary? These two books that will show you just how it's done: *Movie Magic* by Robin Cross (Sterling, 1996) and *Special Effects* by Jake Hamilton (DK Publishing, 1998).

FUN FACT

Dancing Demons

The Chinese tell stories about a kind of zombie called a hopping ghost. An evil spirit occupies a dead body, reanimating it. Because its joints are so stiff, this zombie has to hop to get around, so it can't move very fast. Hopping ghosts smell bad and have very long fingernails that they use for weapons. The hopping ghost is featured in many Chinese films.

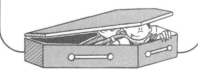

Honor Your Ancestors

People who practice Voodoo honor and respect the spirits of their ancestors. You can, too.

Pick a spirit you would like to honor, such as a relative who has passed away, a favorite pet, or a famous person who is a hero to you. Cover a small table or shelf with a white cloth. Weigh down the four corners of the cloth with stones that you find near your house. Put a glass bowl or jar filled with water in the center of the table; this is where the spirit lives. Also put a jar of earth and a white candle on the table. (Don't light the candle without a grownup's help.)

Place photographs of the person or pet you want to honor on the table, along with things that remind you of the person or animal, such as objects she owned or maybe his favorite food or drink.

From time to time, sit quietly in front of the table and think about the spirit you are honoring and say thank-you for the ways he or she has helped you.

CHAPTER 6

MUMMIES: ALL WRAPPED UP AND NOWHERE TO GO

WORDS to KNOW

mummification: the process of removing all of the moisture from a dead body. Because bacteria need water to survive, *mummification* keeps bacteria from invading the body and prevents it from rotting.

mummy: from the Arabic word *mumiyah,* which refers to a body preserved using wax. The term was incorrectly applied to Egyptian mummies, since they weren't preserved this way.

FuN FACT

Ancient History

Mummies are displayed in many museums around the world, so you can see a mummy yourself, if you want. The best collections are in the British Museum in London and the Egyptian Museum in Cairo. The Museum of Man in San Diego, California, has the largest collection in the United States; it displays Egyptian and Peruvian mummies.

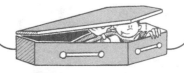

What Are Mummies?

A mummy is a dead body that has been preserved in some way so it doesn't rot. When living things die, bacteria eat them, which makes them break down or decay. **Mummification** protects the body from decaying.

Accidental Mummies

When you think of a **mummy**, you probably think of the mummies of ancient Egypt. But did you know that a body can be mummified naturally, if all the conditions are right? These "accidental" mummies can last for thousands of years. They are important discoveries, because scientists examine them to learn how people used to live, what they ate, what diseases they had, and what they looked like.

Q: Why was the mummy so tense?

A: He was all wound up.

An accidental mummy is a person who happened to die in a place where the environmental conditions kept the body from decaying naturally. Accidental mummies have been found in very hot places buried in sand and in very

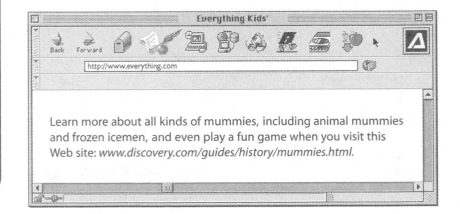

Everything Kids'

http://www.everything.com

Learn more about all kinds of mummies, including animal mummies and frozen icemen, and even play a fun game when you visit this Web site: *www.discovery.com/guides/history/mummies.html.*

cold places buried in ice. They have also been found in mountain caves, where the cool dry air mummified the bodies.

The first Egyptian mummies were very likely accidents. In the desert, it is very hot and dry, so a body buried in the sand could easily become mummified. Most of Egypt is desert, and the ancient Egyptians very likely buried their dead in the sand and later unearthed the mummified bodies. That is probably how the Egyptians got the idea for mummifying people on purpose.

Egyptian Mummies

The Egyptians believed that after people died, they would need their bodies in the next life. They thought that the body was the home of the spirit, called the Ka, which lived on after death. The spirit needed to keep its body as a place to rest. If the body was destroyed, then the Ka might become lost. The Egyptians wanted to preserve the bodies so they would still look lifelike, so they invented a way to preserve the body by mummifying it.

The Egyptians believed that people not only needed their bodies after they died, but they also needed lots of other stuff. They buried their dead in elaborate tombs, along with furniture, food, and incredible treasures. Unfortunately, over the

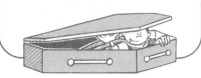

Multicultural Mummies

The ancient Egyptians weren't the only ones who mummified their dead. The native peoples of Peru, the Philippines, and the Canary Islands also preserved bodies through mummification. The oldest mummies are of the Chinchorra people of Peru.

Where in the World?

Egypt is located on the eastern coast of North Africa. On your map, look for the large country bordered by the Mediterranean Sea on the north and the Red Sea on the east. See if you can find the city of Cairo on the Nile River; that's where most ancient (and modern) Egyptians lived.

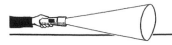 

WORDS to KNOW

pharaohs: the kings of ancient Egypt. *Pharaoh* means "one who lives in the palace." *Pharaohs* were believed to be a living link between humans and the gods.

canopic jars: stone or ceramic jars specially designed to store the *mummy's* organs. The ancient Egyptians believed that anyone who could steal an organ from a *canopic jar* would gain the power to cast evil spells.

Clever Cure

Salt curing is the oldest form of food preservation. Meat, fish, and nuts are coated in salt to draw the moisture out of the food. This process keeps the food from spoiling, because the bacteria that rot food don't have the moisture they need to keep living. Salt-preserved food can last for many years.

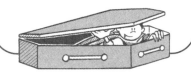

centuries, grave robbers broke into the tombs and stole everything of value, so very little is left for us to study.

Mummification in Egypt started around the year 3200 B.C. The Egyptians loved making mummies. It is estimated that they made 70 million mummies over the course of 3,000 years.

Mummification was very expensive, however, so most people couldn't afford it. Most of the mummies discovered in Egypt had been royalty, such as **pharaohs**, members of the nobility, and high government officials.

How Mummies Are Made

Mummification is a special process that removes all the moisture from a dead body. The dried-out body could stay preserved for a very long time. The process was so good that a lot of mummies still exist today. Many are on display in museums.

The mummification process took seventy days. It was important for specially trained priests to conduct the procedure, otherwise the mummy wouldn't last as long.

The first step was to remove all the internal organs. The soft organs decay rapidly and might spoil the corpse. The stomach, liver, lungs, and intestines were preserved separately in special jars called **canopic jars** that were buried with the mummy. There were four jars, one for each kind of organ removed from the body. Each organ was associated with a particular Egyptian god; and the god's head was carved into the stopper used to seal the jar.

Q: Where do mummies go for a swim?

A: The Dead Sea.

Next, the body was covered with natron, a special kind of salt that would dry the skin out quickly. At least half of a body's weight is due to water, so a mummy weighs very little. That's a diet idea you don't want to try!

Finally, the priests wrapped the mummy. Each mummy required hundreds of yards of linen. The priests wound long strips of linen around every part of the body. They placed amulets among the wrappings and wrote magical words on some of the linen to protect the dead. They also placed a mask of the person's face between the layers of head wrappings. When the priests were done, they wrapped the shroud in place and secured it with linen strips.

The final step was to place the mummy into its **sarcophagus** and seal it into the tomb. The first mummies were entombed in the great pyramids. Later, mummies were buried in underground tombs in the Valley of the Kings. These tombs were cut deep into the natural rock.

The Mummy's Curse

Because mummies were often buried with valuable treasures and other items, there was a great risk that thieves would break into the tombs and steal everything. The ancient Egyptians had to come up with ways to protect the belongings of their dead. They designed clever tricks to fool thieves, such as plugged passageways, secret doors, and hidden rooms. When those methods failed, they relied on the mummy's curse, a curse inscribed on the tomb warning that anyone who disturbed the mummy would have endless misfortune.

If someone ignores the curse and breaks into the tomb anyway, the mummy will rise from the grave to get revenge and protect its treasures, or so the legends say. In reality, thousands of mummies have been found, and none has come back to life yet.

FUN FACT

Deadly Mummies

A mummy may really be able to kill. In 1999, a German scientist examined forty mummies and found that they contained deadly mold spores that were lethal enough to kill anyone who breathed them. Now, archaeologists are careful to wear special masks when they examine old tombs and mummies.

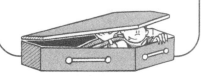

WORDS to KNOW

sarcophagus: a stone coffin. Sometimes the *sarcophagus* was made of gold and silver. It was usually carved and painted to look like the person buried inside.

archaeologist: a scientist who studies the remains of human cultures, such as fossils, artifacts, monuments, and *mummies*. *Archaeologists* try to figure out what the lives and beliefs of ancient peoples were like from what they left behind.

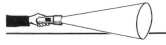
Mumbling Mummy

Fill in the missing letters from
all these words that rhyme with "mummy."

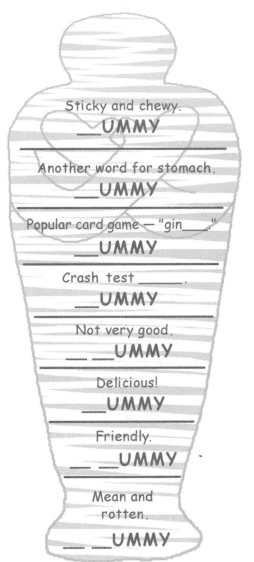

Sticky and chewy.
___ UMMY

Another word for stomach.
___ UMMY

Popular card game — "gin___."
___ UMMY

Crash test _____.
___ UMMY

Not very good.
___ ___ UMMY

Delicious!
___ UMMY

Friendly.
___ ___ UMMY

Mean and rotten.
___ ___ UMMY

King Tut

Since the 1800s, ancient Egypt has fascinated **archaeologists**. These scientists learned a lot about how the Egyptians lived and what their beliefs were just by studying how they buried their dead and the artifacts they left behind in their tombs. The only problem was that most of the tombs had been robbed, so it was very difficult to find a mummy's tomb that still contained anything of value.

One archaeologist, Howard Carter, took up the challenge of finding a full tomb. He believed that there was one tomb that hadn't been found: the tomb of Tutankhamen, or King Tut for short. King Tut ruled Egypt from the age of nine until he died at age eighteen, possibly murdered by one of his trusted advisers. Carter set out on an expedition to find King Tut's final resting place.

He succeeded in 1922. The tomb did contain many fabulous treasures, as well as the mummy of King Tut. But many believed that the tomb was cursed. A legend inscribed over the door was supposed to say: Death shall come on swift wings to him who disturbs the peace of the king. Carter didn't believe in curses, though. So, he removed the treasures and King Tut's mummy. King Tut has since been returned to his tomb, where he lies today.

The curse seemed to come true, though. Lord Carnarvon, the wealthy Englishman who financed the expedition, was the first one to step into the tomb. He died only five months later of a disease contracted from a mosquito bite. The legend says that when Lord Carnarvon died, all the lights in Cairo went out, and Carnarvon's dog back home in England let out a howl and also died. Of the twenty-two people present at the opening of the tomb, six died within the next few years.

However, most of the people who opened King Tut's tomb survived long afterward. The curse didn't appear to work very well. Carter himself was immune to the mummy's curse. He lived to old age and died of natural causes.

The curse was probably only a legend told to frighten grave robbers. The curse's inscription has never been found on King Tut's tomb. But for those who truly believed in it, the curse was all too real!

What did the sign in the Egyptian funeral parlor say?

"Satisfaction guaranteed or double your mummy back."

FuN FACT

Mummy Medicine

Grave robbers who broke into the tombs of mummies weren't just looking for treasure. The mummies themselves were also valuable. During the Middle Ages, countless mummies were destroyed. They were ground up to make magical potions and medicine for stomachaches.

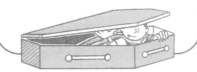

Ready to Read?

Arthur Conan Doyle, the author of the famous Sherlock Holmes stories, also wrote many stories about the supernatural, including some famous stories about reanimated mummies. You can read these stories in *The Supernatural Stories of Arthur Conan Doyle* (Random House, 2000).

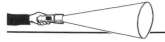

Museum Mystery

Can you help this lost girl find her mummy?

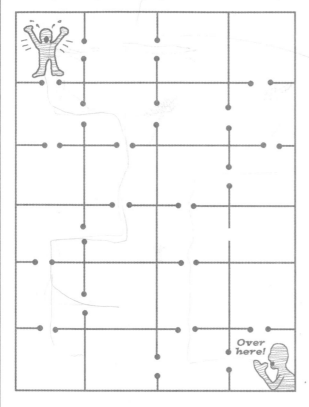

Over here!

66 As for h... who shall destroy this
inscription: he shall not reach his home;
he shall not embrace his children; he shall
not see success. 99

—Real curse found on a mummy's tomb

The Mummy and the *Titanic*

Another legend concerns a mummy's curse and the most famous of all cruise ships, the *Titanic*. In the late 1890s, a young Englishman bought a mummy of an Egyptian princess. He arranged for it to be shipped back to England, but he didn't get home himself. He disappeared on the trip back, never to be found again.

A businessman purchased the mummy next. After suffering a car accident and a house fire, the businessman donated the mummy to the British Museum. But the bad luck didn't stop there. The museum staff reported hearing loud bangs and cries coming from the mummy's sarcophagus at night. Objects were mysteriously thrown around the room where the mummy was on display.

The museum sold the unlucky mummy to an American archaeologist. He had it shipped home on the *Titanic*'s first cruise. And you know what happened to the *Titanic*.

So, did a mummy's curse really cause the most famous shipwreck in history? Well, probably not. There is no record of a mummy carried onboard the *Titanic*. That infamous mummy is still on display in the British Museum, where it rests quietly.

Make an
Apple Mummy

Here's how to make your own mummy.

Ingredients
Small apple
Knife
Plastic cup
$\frac{1}{3}$ cup baking soda
$\frac{1}{3}$ cup table salt

Directions

1. Slice the apple. Or carve the apple to look like a face or a body. (Get an adult's help when you are using a knife.)

2. Put the apple into a plastic cup.

3. Mix the baking soda and salt.

4. Pour this mixture over the apple, making sure it is completely covered.

5. Put the cup on a shelf or in a cabinet out of direct sunlight. Leave it alone for at least a week.

6. Carefully pull the apple out of the salt and baking soda, but don't wash it off. You should have a shrunken apple "mummy."

*This project should be done with adult supervision.

CHAPTER 7
GOLEMS: MONSTERS MADE OF CLAY

Bringing Clay to Life

Golems are artificial men made of clay that are brought to life through magic. The golem is a part of Jewish folklore. In Jewish legend, the golem is a kind of servant.

A golem is a lot like a robot. Although golems look like men, they aren't human. They walk and move jerkily, also like robots. And a golem is never able to speak. The golem doesn't need to eat or sleep, and it performs whatever chores its master, the person who made it, says. Unlike a robot, however, the golem is alive. If it isn't watched carefully, a golem can easily become a monster.

The First Golems

The legend of the golem is very old, going back to biblical times. According to Jewish holy texts, many wise men created golems. Making a golem required extensive knowledge of the Hebrew alphabet and the magical use of the name of God. Only the most gifted Jewish scholars could do it correctly.

The purpose for making the golem had be a pure one, or it could go dangerously wrong. Under no circumstances could a golem be made for an evil purpose, or it would turn into an out-of-control monster. You couldn't even make a golem just to do simple chores around the house; that didn't qualify as a pure purpose. Very special Jewish holy men spent a lot of time studying holy teachings. When they completed their studies, they made a golem. It was like a final exam to show how much they had learned, but they usually destroyed the golem as soon as they had brought it to life.

Q: What's the best way to speak to a golem?

A: From a long way away.

FUN FACT

Golem Robots

Like robots, golems can't really think for themselves. When set to a task, they will continue until they are told to stop. Once a golem was instructed to fill a barrel with water and then left alone. The golem continued to fill the barrel until it overflowed and flooded the house.

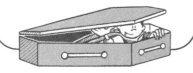

The Famous Golem of Prague

Rabbi Judah Loew of Prague created the most famous golem 400 years ago. Prague is the capital of the Czech Republic, a country in Eastern Europe. The Jewish people lived together in their own neighborhood inside the city.

At that time, many people were prejudiced against the Jewish people, who were often persecuted. They were blamed for crimes they didn't commit and were in danger of being attacked by mobs. Also, they had to work very hard and didn't have much time for fun or to spend with their families.

Rabbi Loew was the most respected **rabbi** in Prague. He wanted to help his people with their problems. So, he decided to create a golem that would protect the Jewish people of Prague. He figured that the golem could patrol the Jewish neighborhood at night and perform chores during the day. Since Loew was a well-educated rabbi, he knew exactly how to make a golem.

Rabbi Loew was pleased with how well his golem worked and protected the Jewish neighborhood. But he wanted to teach the golem how to act more human. This knowledge made the golem dissatisfied. It wanted to be a real person. It became angry and ran amok, throwing rocks and breaking windows.

FUN FACT

How Hungry!

Rabbi Loew was always trying to teach his golem how to act more human. One day, he decided to teach the golem how to eat by showing it how to chew and swallow bread. The golem thought anything could be eaten, not just food. One day, it ate a whole brick!

Where in the World?

Prague is the capital of the Czech Republic. To find Prague on a map, first locate the continent of Europe and then the country of Germany. Move your finger east. The Czech Republic borders Germany on the east. Prague is located in the northeastern part of the country.

Rabbi Loew knew that his golem had become too dangerous. The golem could no longer control its anger and might hurt someone. So, the rabbi destroyed the golem. He put the clay body in the attic of his synagogue, where it supposedly still lies to this day.

The Life of a Golem

Only someone with an in-depth knowledge of the Jewish religion can successfully make a golem. The **Kabbalah**, a Jewish holy book, provides the instructions. The Kabbalah describes the system of Jewish magic. Only by studying the Kabbalah and the Jewish texts can a person unlock the secrets of creation and create a man from clay. The process has to be performed without any mistakes, though, or it won't work.

How to Make a Golem

Making a golem requires three people: a learned rabbi and two helpers. All three must have ritually cleaned themselves before starting the process, and they must wear pure white robes.

At night, the three make the clay for the golem. They must take the soil from a place where no man has dug, and then knead the soil with pure spring water until it forms clay. They use this clay to fashion the likeness of a man.

Once the clay figure has been made, the rabbi walks clockwise around the clay man seven times, chanting special magical formulas derived from the Kabbalah. These formulas use the Hebrew alphabet in a particular way. If the rabbi does not chant the

66 The story of the Golem serves as a cautionary tale about the limits of human power . . . as the fields of computer science, robotics, and gene manipulation advance, technological Golems may arise in our culture. 99

—From *Golem* by David Wisniewski (Clarion Books, 1996)

Q: Is it true that Frankenstein's monster can't hurt you if you're carrying a torch?

A: Depends on how fast you carry it.

complicated formulas exactly right, the spell won't work, and the golem won't come to life.

If every part of the ritual has been performed correctly, the golem's body begins to glow red. Long hair grows all over the body, and the golem's fingers and toes grow nails. The golem is then alive. It can walk and work, but it can't talk.

To finish the process of bringing the golem to life, the rabbi writes the **Hebrew** word *emet* on the golem's forehead. In Hebrew, *emet* means "truth." Each day, the rabbi must place a clay tablet or a piece of paper under the golem's tongue. Written on the paper or tablet are the golem's instructions for what it must do that day. If the rabbi forgets to put the tablet or paper under the golem's tongue, life will leave the golem, and it will revert to clay.

Why Golems Attack

When the golem is first brought to life, it is a faithful servant. It performs whatever chores its creator tells it to without question. But the golem does not remain that way. Every day, it grows a little bigger and stronger. The more time it spends with people, the more it wants to become a person itself. And it

תמא
Tav Mem Alef
"emet"

Everything Kids'

http://www.everything.com

Does the golem story seem familiar to you? Perhaps it reminds you of the story of Pinocchio. You can read *Pinocchio* and several other classic novels at *www.classicreader.com/toc.php/sid.3*.

FUN FACT

Giant Golem

One rabbi let his golem grow too large. He could no longer reach the golem's forehead, and therefore, he couldn't destroy it. The rabbi commanded the golem to stoop so he could reach its forehead and erase the first letter. The golem immediately turned to clay and collapsed on top of the rabbi, crushing him.

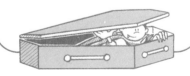

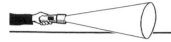

Basic Ingredients

Follow the directions to turn each of these raw materials into a living creature! Use your magic to figure out which letters to add, subtract, or change. As you change each word, write it down on the lines provided.

1. Use **STONE** to create something that slithers.

   (switch 2nd and 4th letters, then change two letters) _____

2. Use **CEMENT** to make creatures that stand upright.

   (delete three letters) _____

3. Use **CLAY** to make a creature that lives in two shells.

   (change one letter) _____

4. Use **WOOD** to make a creature that howls at the moon.

   (change two letters) _____

5. Use **ICE** to make creatures that squeak.

   (add one letter) _____

6. Use **SNOW** to make a creature that flies in the night.

   (delete two letters, then add one letter) _____

grows frustrated because it knows it will never really be human.

When the golem becomes too big, strong, and angry, it is dangerous. It can't control its anger and hurts others with its great strength. The golem's creator is usually in the most danger. In its frustration, the golem often turns on its creator.

Golems must only be created for pure purposes, such as helping others. If a golem is made for an evil reason, such as to hurt others or to get revenge, its creator is much more

likely to lose control. Even using the golem for selfish reasons, such as to do the work for a lazy rabbi, will ensure that the golem will grow larger and become more likely to attack its creator.

Getting Rid of a Golem

Because golems are made of clay, they are practically indestructible. If you tried to attack them, you probably wouldn't even make a dent! That's why golems make such good protectors.

> **Q:** How can you tell Dr. Frankenstein had a good sense of humor?
>
> **A:** He kept his monster in stitches.

There is one sure way to get rid of a golem. The rabbi must change the word *emet* written on the golem's forehead to the word *met* by erasing the first letter. In Hebrew, *met* means "death." Once that is done, life will immediately leave the golem, and it will become clay again.

Unfortunately, it's not always that easy. If the golem has grown too large or too strong, it may be impossible to get close enough to change the word on its forehead. That's why anyone who makes a golem must be very careful to destroy the golem before it gets out of hand.

Are These Golems?

Any **inanimate** object that is brought to life through magic or science can be considered a golem. The object doesn't have to be made of clay or animated in the manner described in the Kabbalah. Even objects brought to life using scientific means can be kinds of golems.

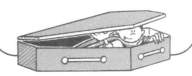

An Odd Lunch

Golems don't have to be men; they can also be animals. Once, two rabbis were hungry. They made a calf out of clay and brought it to life just so they could eat it.

inanimate: not alive. An *inanimate* object cannot think for itself. Look around. Can you name some things that are inanimate? What would they be like if they were alive?

WORDS to KNOW

cloning: using a person's DNA to create another person who is identical to the first. The *clone* is like the original person's identical twin. Scientists may soon have the power to create human life through *cloning*.

What do you call a team of Frankenstein-monsters that plays football?

The All-Scars!

Ready to Read?

The original Frankenstein story is very different from the movies. If you'd like to try reading the story for yourself, find the Great Illustrated Classics edition (Abdo and Daughters, 2000).

Frankenstein's Monster

Everybody is familiar with the story of Frankenstein's monster. Mary Shelley first told this story in her novel *Frankenstein*. Frankenstein's monster has since made an appearance in so many books, movies, and TV shows that he has become one of the most popular monsters around.

In the story, Dr. Frankenstein has an obsession: to create new life. He assembles a complete body out of body parts stolen from local graveyards and then uses lightning to bring that body to life in the form of a hideous monster. But his experiment backfires when Frankenstein loses control of his creation, and the monster kills all the people the doctor loves.

The story told in *Frankenstein* is very similar to the story of the golem. Like the golem, Frankenstein's monster is big, strong, and can't speak (at least, not at first). The monster also longs to be human, becomes angry, and loses control. Since Mary Shelley was very familiar with German folk stories, she was probably aware of the golem legend when she wrote *Frankenstein* and used it as a basis for her novel.

As we move to the possibility of **cloning** real animals today, it is important to remember the moral of both stories: Humans should not "play God" and create life, because we can all too easily lose control of our creations and end up making monsters.

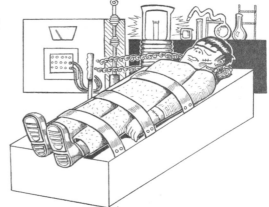

Make Clay Monsters

Using modeling clay and scraps of things you have around your house, make your own clay monsters. Scout around the house for little bits of things to complete your monster. Make sure everything you use is oven-safe, because you're going to bake your monster. So you can't use plastic that will melt or anything that will burn.

Ingredients

Modeling clay in assorted colors (you can buy polymer clay in a hobby store). You can use:

- Aluminum foil
- Bolts
- Bottle caps
- Coins
- Glass beads
- Keys
- Marbles
- Nuts
- Paper clips
- Pins
- Screws
- Springs
- Thumbtacks
- Anything else that will make your monster particularly monstrous

Directions

1. Roll off a marble-size piece of clay and shape it into a monster's body. Be creative: make bug shapes, lizard shapes, or weird alien shapes!
2. Stick the decorations into the clay to complete your monsters. You can make teeth, eyes, legs, ears, tails, hair, and weird noses or whatever. See just how strange you can make your monsters look.

To preserve your monsters, get a grownup to help you bake them (this only works with polymer clay, so check the package).

1. Heat the oven to 275 degrees.
2. Put your monsters into a glass baking dish.
3. Bake for up to twenty minutes, checking them often.

Let the monsters cool before you touch them. Now you have an army of clay monsters of your own.

CHAPTER 8

GIANTS: MONSTERS OF MYTH

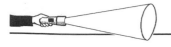 
Who Were the Giants?

Legends about **giants** have been told in countries all around the world, from Ireland to Japan. Giants are enormous humans, ranging from 10 feet to 100 feet tall or more. Besides having great size and strength, they usually had magical powers.

Giants also often had too many body parts. For instance, they might have several heads, arms, or eyes.

Everyone agrees that there aren't any real giants (except for maybe some basketball players). But stories about giants have been told for thousands of years. Giants are important characters in the mythology, folklore, and fairy tales of many countries. Stories about giants were often used to explain natural events that ancient people didn't understand. For instance, thunder was the sound of giants bellowing, and earthquakes were caused by their heavy footsteps. Fire-breathing giants buried underground made volcanoes erupt when they got angry.

Giants in Greek Mythology

In Greek mythology, giants were created before people and even before the gods. These giants, called **Titans**, were the children of Gaia, the earth, and Uranus, the sky. They were born when Uranus's blood fell upon the earth.

Uranus hid his giant children because he was afraid of their great strength and power. With the help of their mother, the Titans overthrew Uranus and ruled the earth in a time of peace. They helped to create much of the universe, including the first people.

There were twelve Titans: six men and six women. Each Titan married one of his sisters and had children. The children of the Titan **Cronus** were the Greek gods. Cronus knew that his children were fated to overthrow him, just as he had helped defeat his own father.

WORDS to KNOW

giant: from the word *gigantus,* which means "gigantic." A *giant* is a legendary human being of great size and strength who sometimes also has extraordinary powers.

titan: someone of great size or strength or someone who has done great things. The word *titanic* means huge. No wonder the largest cruise ship ever built was named the *Titanic.*

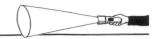
To prevent his children from going to war against him, Cronus swallowed them. His wife wasn't happy about this, so she saved one of her children, the great god Zeus. She gave Cronus a stone to swallow instead and raised Zeus in secrecy. When he grew up, Zeus tricked his father into throwing up his brothers and sisters. United, they went to war against the Titans. They defeated the Titans and buried them far beneath the earth.

Another group of Greek giants was the Cyclops. These giants had only one eye in the middle of their foreheads. When they were born, their father, Uranus, imprisoned them because he was afraid of their great strength. In the war against the Titans, Zeus released the Cyclops. They were skilled metal-workers, and they made thunderbolts for Zeus to use as weapons. They lived in Mount Aetna, a volcano in Sicily, Italy, that smoked constantly from their active forge.

The descendants of the first Cyclops were shepherds who lived on remote islands and ate human flesh. A famous Greek soldier named Odysseus was sailing home after a long war when he encountered a Cyclops. Odysseus's men were hungry, so they landed on an island to look for food. They found a cave full of sheep, but they belonged to a one-eyed giant. The Cyclops trapped the men in the cave by rolling a boulder across the entrance.

WORDS to KNOW

Cronus: The Titan associated with time. Several English words related to time contain the prefix *chrono-*, which is derived from the name *Cronus,* including *chronograph, chronology,* and *chronicle.* A lot of people use chronographs everyday. Of course, we call them watches!

odyssey: a long, adventurous journey. Odysseus was famous in Greek mythology for making a ten-year sea voyage and having many adventures along the way.

FUN FACT

A Heavy Load

One of the Titans was named Atlas. After being defeated by the gods, Atlas was punished by being forced to carry the sky on his shoulders for all time. Later, the serpent-haired Medusa turned Atlas to stone. Mount Atlas is located in Africa in the spot where Atlas stood, holding up the sky.

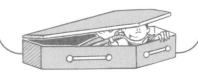

Odysseus was very clever, and he came up with a plan to escape. He tricked the Cyclops into drinking too much wine. Once the Cyclops fell asleep, Odysseus blinded him. The Cyclops couldn't see to find the men. Eventually, he rolled the boulder away from the cave entrance to let his sheep out to graze. As he did so, he felt along their backs for Odysseus's men. But Odysseus's men clung to the bellies of the sheep instead and that's how they escaped.

Giants in Norse Mythology

The people of Norway, Sweden, and Denmark also told myths about giants. As in many other cultures, giants in Norse mythology were associated with the forces of nature. They were the **personification** of these forces. Because the ocean, weather, earthquakes, and volcanoes were so much more powerful than people, giants were invented to explain their awesome force.

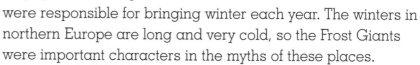

There were several kinds of giants in Norse mythology. The most common were the Frost Giants. They had hair, beards, and fingernails made of icicles, and they exhaled ice particles when they spoke. These giants were responsible for bringing winter each year. The winters in northern Europe are long and very cold, so the Frost Giants were important characters in the myths of these places.

Just as in Greek mythology, the Norse giants were the parents of the gods. The gods and the giants had a big war. Ymir, the father of the Frost Giants, was killed in this war, and his body was used to make the earth.

FUN FACT

Early Archaeology

Five thousand years ago, the ancient Greeks found skulls of what they thought were Cyclops. Actually, they were the skulls of elephants! The Greeks thought that the nasal cavity opening for the trunk was the Cyclops' one eye.

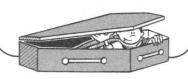

WORDS to KNOW

personification: an object or an idea that is given human form. For example, a giant who is the *personification* of the ocean might have hair made of seaweed and live at the bottom of the sea. What other qualities would this *personification* have?

Awesome!

Fit these scrambled REALLY BIG words into the criss-cross grid. When you've finished the puzzle correctly, you can read down the shaded column to find another big word. HINT: We left you a helpful G-I-A-N-T!

MUEROOSN _____

EISMMNE _____

UTENEDSROM _____

EVAMISS _____

ICNGGIAT _____

WGEOIRTN _____

CSLSOOAL _____

HUEG _____

STVA _____

"This guy is GARGANTUAN!"

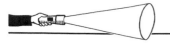 
Giants in British Folklore

Legends say that giants lived in England, Wales, and Ireland before people did. When the first people arrived, they had to battle the giants to take over the land. These giants are associated with the rock formations and ancient stone rings found in Britain. One stone formation in Cornwall is called Stonehenge, or the Giant's Dance. According to the stories, the stones were once giants who were frozen as God's punishment for dancing in a meadow on Sunday.

The giants helped shape the earth, according to the legends. Winding valleys and mountain hollows were their trails. The giants' footprints became lakebeds. They threw massive boulders and raised solitary hills. In fact, giants were said to be responsible for any natural formation that could not be easily explained.

One British giant, measuring 240 feet in height, supposedly left his form on Somerset Hill, which is where he fell when he died. His muscles, skin, and bones dissolved, leaving a vast human silhouette sunk into the earth. The local people call him the Long Man of Wilmington.

Q: What goes ha-ha-ha-ha-THUD?

A: A giant laughing its head off.

Where in the World?

Where do the Norse giants come from? Locate the continent of Europe on a map. Find the area far in the north that juts down into the North Sea like a curved finger. The eastern part of that land is Norway, and the western part is Sweden. Denmark juts up from the continent of Europe beneath Norway and Sweden.

Ready to Read?

To read about the giants for yourself, get the book *English Fairy Tales* (Everyman's Library Children's Classics, 1993). Inside, you'll find not just giants, but also ghosts, fairies, wicked stepmothers, and other monsters.

Many giant legends come from an area of England called Cornwall. Read these stories for yourself by going to *www.perseus.tufts.edu/ Herakles/giants.html*.

Depending on where they lived, the ancient giants of the United Kingdom had very different personalities. The English giants were all evil. The Welsh giants were clever and cunning. The Irish giants, called the Fomorians, were actually quite nice.

Q: Why did the Cyclops have to close the school?

A: He only had one pupil.

The most famous British giant of all was Gogmagog. In ancient times, he was the leader of the British giants. Brutus, the legendary founder of Great Britain, had to fight him. The giants were fond of wrestling, so Brutus challenged Gogmagog to a wrestling match. He won and erected a statue of Gogmagog in the Guildhall of the London merchants to commemorate the giant's defeat.

Giants also appear in many British fairy tales. These giants were often stupid, greedy, and fond of eating people. Usually, the only way to defeat these giants was to trick them. Jack was a famous giant-killer of the fairy tales who was particularly good at tricking giants.

FUN FACT

Jolly Giant

Paul Bunyan was a good-natured giant of American folklore. When he walked across the country, he left gigantic footsteps. They filled with rain, creating the thousand lakes of Minnesota. Paul Bunyan also scooped out the Great Lakes to get water for his blue ox, Babe.

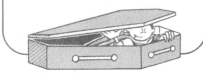

Super Sized

Unscramble the following BIG words and write them on the lines provided. To each one, add a word from the box to make a familiar word or phrase about something that isn't small at all!

SQUID   MARKET   DANE
CANYON   SHOT   JET

1. **IGB** _____

2. **BMUOJ** _____

3. **DAGRN** _____

4. **UPRES** _____

5. **NAITG** _____

6. **ERTGA** _____

The Big Picture

See what is lurking in your neighborhood by following these directions:

1. Find box 1-A and copy it into square 1-A in the grid.
2. Find box 1-B and copy it into square 1-B in the grids.
3. Continue doing this until you've copied all the boxes into the grid.

	A	B	C	D	E
1					
2					
3					
4					
5					
6					

continued

FuN FACT

Southwestern Giants

In 1911, miners were digging out layers of guano from a cave in Nevada when they found the mummified remains of a person who was 6½ feet tall. The mummy had distinctly red hair. Could this have been one of the Si-te-cah giants?

❝ Jack traveled the country around,
East, west, north, and south, far and near,
Abroad or at home he was found
Where he of a giant could hear. ❞

—From the fairy tale
Jack the Giant-Killer

Giants in Native American Folklore

Native Americans have lots of stories about giants. Just as in the Norse and Greek myths, the giants of Native American legends were associated with natural forces. The Native Americans believed that the giants were the first race to live on earth, long before people made an appearance.

The Iroquois tell legends of the Chenoo, clumsy giants made of stone who frequently fought among themselves. They uprooted trees to use as clubs and hurled boulders at each other. Despite their size, the Chenoo were afraid of people and would blend into the rocks to **camouflage** themselves whenever people came near. Only the Native American shamans could see them. The shamans used magical spells to enslave the Chenoo.

The ancient legends of the Paiute describe a race of red-haired giants called the Si-te-cahs. These giants were the enemies of many Native American tribes in the southwestern United States.

Q: What happened to the giant who took the five o'clock train home?

A: He had to give it back.

Odious Ogres

Ogres are a particularly evil kind of giant. They aren't quite as large as the other giants, but they are several feet taller and much broader than a man. They are also much stronger. Ogres are very cruel and vicious, even more so than the other giants.

Ogres smell horrible, like rotting meat. They have wart-covered, twisted faces, and their bodies are matted with bristly black hair. Unfortunately, they like to snack on people! The good news is that they aren't very smart and can easily be fooled by the people they try to catch and eat.

Write a Monster Story

Pick a monster from this book or make up your own, and write a story about it. To get started, answer these questions:

- What does the monster look like? (You might want to draw a picture of it.)

- How does the monster act? Is it scary or mischievous? (Perhaps it's scared of people!)

- What kinds of sounds does the monster make: growls, roars, evil laughs, groans, or whistles?

- Where does the monster come from? Where does it live now?

- What does the monster eat?

- How can the monster be stopped or killed? Remember, killing a monster often requires a special weapon or magical spell.

- What would happen if you ran into the monster? How would you get away?

CHAPTER 9

BIGFOOT: THE MYSTERIOUS APEMAN

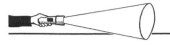

Bigfoot Around the World

For thousands of years, the natives of isolated places like the high mountains of Asia and the wild forests of northwestern North America have told legends about a creature that is half-man, half-ape. This creature was tall, broad, and covered with hair. It was also so shy that it was rarely spotted. The monster went by many different names:

- **Almas** in China
- **Bigfoot** in the northwestern United States
- **Chuchuna** in Siberia
- **Sasquatch** in Canada
- **Skunk-ape** in Florida
- **Yeti** in the Himalaya Mountains of Nepal and Tibet
- **Yowie** in Australia

WORDS to KNOW

abominable snowman: The natives of Nepal call the yeti *meh-teh kangmi,* which means "man-like thing that is not a man." The first Western explorers incorrectly translated this as *abominable snowman.* Newspapers picked up the nickname, and it stuck.

Many Homes, One Monster

Although these creatures have been spotted in many different parts of the world, they are all remarkably similar. They all live in remote areas: high mountains, dense forests, or overgrown swamps. All of the creatures are very big, between seven and twelve feet tall, with broad shoulders and long arms. They have a face like an ape with a flat nose and yellow eyes. They are covered in thick fur that is red, brown, black, white, or gray. And they all smell terrible, like a cross between a skunk and a wet dog.

It doesn't seem as if the **abominable snowman** can talk, but it may be able to communicate with others of its species. It makes many different sounds, including whistles, grunts, screams,

What are the most popular bedtime stories for baby monsters?

"Little Boo Creep" and "Moldy Locks"

Q: What do you get when you cross Bigfoot with a vegetable?

A: A sasquash.

howls, and roars. These sounds have been recorded, but no one can say whether it was the creature or some other animal.

The creature doesn't appear to be particularly dangerous. Usually, it seems scared of people, hiding from them or watching them curiously from a distance. It can move very quickly through snow or over rocks, so it can get away easily when a person comes too close.

Bigfoot, or the Sasquatch

Bigfoot lives in remote areas of the U.S. Pacific Northwest and across the border in Canada. The Native Americans and Native Canadians who live in the area have many stories about this creature, which they call **Sasquatch.**

The first American and Canadian explorers also encountered Bigfoot. In 1811, a trader named David Thompson was crossing the Rocky Mountains in Canada. He kept a daily journal, in which he wrote about some tracks he had found. They looked like human footprints, but they were bigger and had only four toes. His journal is the first written record of Bigfoot.

In 1924, a gold prospector named Albert Ostman had a close encounter with Bigfoot. He was looking for gold in British Columbia. One night while he was sleeping, something picked

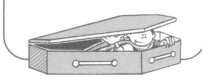

Protected Creatures

In Skamania County in Washington State, it is illegal to kill a Bigfoot. Anyone who does has to pay a fine of $1,000 and may be sentenced to up to five years in jail. The Sioux have also forbidden the hunting of Bigfoot on their land.

Sasquatch: meaning "wild man of the woods." *Sasquatch* is the name given to Bigfoot by the native tribes of British Columbia, Canada. The legends of many Native American tribes mention Bigfoot.

To read more about the legend of the yeti, go to *http://legendofyeti.com*. At that site, you can download yeti wallpaper for your computer and play games.

him up and carried him almost 25 miles through the woods. When he awoke, a family of Sasquatches surrounded him. They didn't hurt the prospector, but they did keep him prisoner for six days, until he managed to escape.

In 1958, a road crew working in northwest California found enormous footprints in the mud around their work site. They took pictures and plaster casts of the footprints, and the story was published in many newspapers. The creature was nicknamed "Bigfoot" because of the size of its footprints, and the name stuck.

> **Q:** Where are yetis found?
>
> **A:** They're so big; they're hardly ever lost.

The Yeti

The yeti makes its home in the high snowfields of the Himalaya Mountains. For thousands of years, the locals have told stories about these apemen. When people from Europe and America began to explore the mountains in the 1800s, they brought back similar stories. They had also glimpsed the yeti or found its huge footprints in the snow.

In 1921 C. K. Howard-Bury, a well-respected mountain climber, took the first photographs of the yeti's footprints. He found the footprints high up the slope of Mount Everest. Other mountain climbers also came across footprints or spotted the yeti from a distance. In 1937, plaster casts were taken of the yeti's footprints. The tracks were 14 inches long and 7 inches wide.

Where in the World?

The Himalaya Mountains extend 1,550 miles through the Asian countries of India, Nepal, and Tibet. In Nepal, they cover three-quarters of the land and contain nine of the world's tallest mountains, including Mount Everest. The yeti's footprints have been found 21,000 feet up Mount Everest.

Ready to Read?

To learn more about the famous explorer who first climbed to the top of one of the world's highest mountains, read *Triumph on Everest: A Photobiography of Sir Edmund Hillary* by Broughton Coburn (National Geographic Society, 2000).

They sank deep into the snow, showing that the creature that made them was very big and heavy.

Sir Edmund Hillary was the first man to climb to the top of Mount Everest. He had heard the stories and wanted to see a yeti for himself. He made many expeditions, but he never saw the yeti. Still, he brought back a skull that he had borrowed from a monastery in Nepal, which he claimed was a yeti's skull. The skull was 300 years old. But when scientists studied it, they found that it was the skull of a mountain goat.

In 1961, the government of Nepal declared that the yeti officially existed. The yeti has become their national symbol. It is also an important source of income, since many tourists go to Nepal each year in the hopes of seeing a yeti.

Who Is Bigfoot?

Scientists and others have come up with many **theories** to explain what Bigfoot actually is. Many scientists think that Bigfoot doesn't exist at all. Despite all of the sightings and footprints, there is still no definite evidence that Bigfoot is real. No one has ever captured Bigfoot alive or found a skeleton that scientists can study.

Lack of Evidence

People who believe in Bigfoot have many theories to explain why there is no concrete evidence of the creature's existence. They point out that Bigfoot is always seen in remote areas where few people live. Over the years, Bigfoot learned to be afraid of people. It hides from people, doesn't come out much during the daytime, and never stays long in one place, which is why it is so rarely seen.

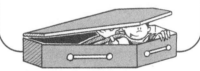

The Wanderer

How did Bigfoot end up in so many places? Bigfoot seems to be a nomadic creature that wanders from place to place with no real home. A long time ago, the Bigfoot species could have walked from Siberia to North America over a land bridge, just as the Native Americans did.

theory: a guess about something based on limited knowledge. Scientists come up with theories to explain what they don't understand, and then they conduct experiments to prove or disprove their *theories*.

Some people think that Bigfoot comes from another world, traveling back and forth between our world and its own. Others think that Bigfoot is an alien experiment. The aliens let Bigfoot run loose for a while and then fly it away in their spaceships. What do you think of these theories?

The only real evidence of Bigfoot is footprints, stories of sightings, and a few blurry photographs. An ordinary animal, like a bear or an ape, could have made the footprints. The footprints are usually found in mud or snow, which could spread or melt to make the tracks appear bigger than they actually are.

The footprints don't all look the same, either. Some have three toes, some have four, and some have five. On some tracks, the toes are different sizes, and on others, they are the same size. Because the footprints aren't all the same, they can't be used to prove that Bigfoot exists.

Sightings of Bigfoot can be explained away as mistaken identity. Because Bigfoot is usually seen at a distance in snowstorms, among the trees, or at night, it's easy to see how someone could make a mistake. Many scientists think that Bigfoot is actually a known animal, like a grizzly bear walking upright.

Until someone actually finds a living Bigfoot or a skeleton, scientists won't accept that there is such a creature. The hunt for more conclusive evidence is underway.

Putting Us On: Bigfoot Hoaxes

Over the years, many photographs have been taken of Bigfoot and its cousins around the world. Photographs and plaster casts have also been made of the footprints that Bigfoot left behind. But many pieces of evidence have turned out to be **hoaxes**.

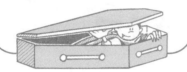

The Big Search

Groups of Bigfoot hunters are actively searching for evidence that Bigfoot exists. One such group is the Bigfoot Field Researchers Organization (*www.bfro.net/*). They collect reports of sightings and try to solve the mystery of who Bigfoot really is.

hoax: something fake and often ridiculous that is passed off as real. *Hoax* probably comes from the word *hocus,* as in the phrase *hocus-pocus.*

Q: What do you get if you cross the abominable snowman with a vampire?

A: Frostbite.

Follow Those Footprints

More people have seen Bigfoot's footprints than have seen the monster itself! See if you can find the trail that leads to the shy sasquatch.

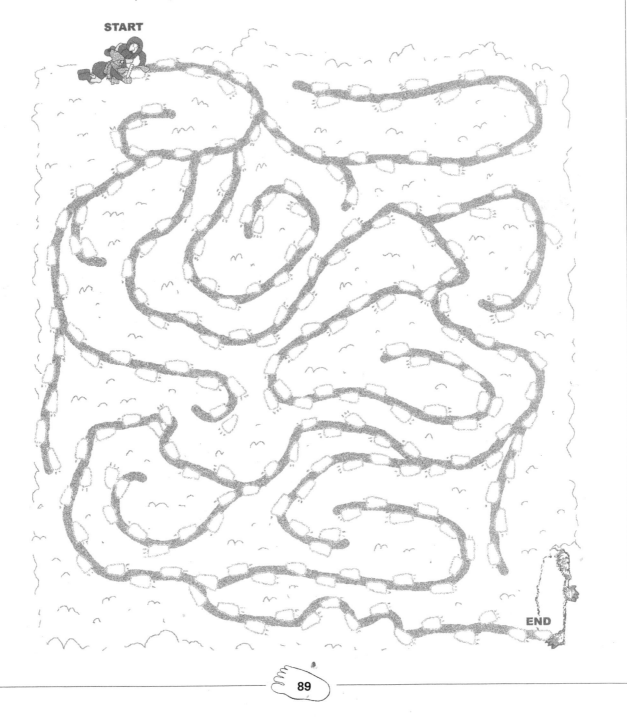

START

END

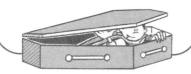

Fact or Fiction?

Many other animals that were long thought to be myths have turned out to actually exist. These include the mountain gorilla and the giant panda, which also live in remote areas. Both animals were only "discovered" by Westerners in the early 1900s, even though natives had told stories about them for hundreds of years.

People have made Bigfoot footprints using fake wooden feet and altered boots. One company even sells a set of oversize plastic strap-on feet that you can use to fool your friends and family.

The most controversial piece of evidence is a film of Bigfoot shot in 1967 in California by Roger Patterson and Bill Gimlin. You've probably either seen this film on TV or seen photographs taken from it. Even many years later, people still debate whether the film is real or a hoax.

Some people claim that the Bigfoot in the film is a man in an ape suit. The film was taken about the same time a movie was made. The theory is that the man who designed the ape costumes for *Planet of the Apes* also made the Bigfoot costume for this film. He won an Oscar for his work on the movie, so he was very good at creating realistic ape costumes.

Others say that the film can't be a fake, because the Bigfoot walks in a way that no person ever could. Perhaps the film was shot at a slower speed and then speeded up later. That could make the Bigfoot appear to move in an impossible way.

We might never know if this film was a hoax. When Roger Patterson died, he was still insisting that it was real. But another

❝ I can't help thinking that somewhere in the universe there has to be something better than man. Has to be. ❞

—From the movie
Planet of the Apes
(20th Century Fox, 1968)

man claimed that he witnessed the hoax. Again, more evidence is needed before we can decide whether the film is proof that Bigfoot exists.

Why would so many people play hoaxes? Some people want to make money selling their stories. Others want to be famous and have their pictures in the newspaper. Some just have fun seeing what they can get people to believe. It's a good idea to investigate suspicious Bigfoot reports carefully so you don't get fooled.

Not all of the evidence can be faked, though. There have been too many sightings in very different parts of the world by very different kinds of people. Everyone can't be in on the hoax!

Hink Pinks

The answer to Hink Pinks are rhyming words, both with the same number of syllables.

1. Nickname for a girl sasquatch named Elizabeth.

   _____ _____

2. Cart used by a monster that breathes fire.

   _____ _____

3. Fake monster wrapped in linen.

   _____ _____

4. Just one big mean goblin.

   _____ _____

5. Serious monster made of clay.

   _____ _____

What happened to the monster who ate the electric company?

He went into shock!

Identify Animal Tracks

Finding and identifying animal tracks is one of humankind's oldest skills. See if you can find and identify animal tracks for yourself. Maybe you'd make a good Bigfoot hunter!

First, find a place where there are likely to be animal tracks. A good spot is the muddy bank of a stream in the woods or in a park. Check the mud carefully for tracks. You might see the tracks of dogs, cats, deer, raccoons, squirrels, opossums, or birds. A book showing pictures of animal tracks will help you identify them.

To preserve the tracks, make a plaster cast. You'll need some water, plaster of Paris, a tin can, a strip of cardboard, and tape.

1. Gently brush all the twigs, leaves, and pebbles away from around the track.
2. Roll the cardboard strip into a tube just big enough to fit around the track, and tape the ends together.
3. Press the cardboard strip into the mud around the track. That will be the mold to hold the plaster of Paris.

4. Mix the plaster of Paris and water in the tin can until it is the consistency of pancake batter.
5. Pour the mixture onto the track, until it hits the cardboard tube.
6. Let it harden for 30 minutes. Then, lift it off the ground and peel off the cardboard strip. You should have a perfect impression of the track you've found.

MONSTERS OF LAKES AND SEAS

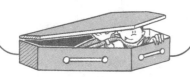

Lake Monsters

Lake monsters live all over the world, but they all look remarkably alike. They have huge black bodies with two or three humps, slender necks about 6 feet long, and tiny, calf-like heads. They are estimated to be at least 30 feet long.

Nessie, the Monster of Loch Ness

The most famous of all the lake monsters is the Loch Ness Monster, affectionately nicknamed Nessie. Loch Ness, in Scotland, is the largest freshwater lake in the United Kingdom. It is 24 miles long and has an average depth of 450 feet. At some points, it plunges down 1,000 feet.

The water of Loch Ness is cold and murky, and there are dangerous currents. It is impossible to see more than a few feet under the surface. Lots of fish live in the lake, so there is plenty to eat. Loch Ness is the ideal place for a gigantic lake monster to hide.

The earliest recorded sighting of the Loch Ness Monster was in the year 565, which would make Nessie 1,500 years old. Or, there may be twenty or thirty monsters in the lake that are breeding. With that many Nessies around, you'd think they would be spotted more often.

In 1933, a road was built around the lake. As more people started traveling around the lake, the number of reported sightings went up suddenly. A famous photograph of Nessie was taken in 1934. It was later proved to be a hoax, however. The photo was actually of a small model floating in the water.

In 1972, a team of scientists tried to prove Nessie's existence. They used a sonar device equipped with a camera to take underwater pictures automatically when objects were detected. One picture showed what appeared to be a large diamond-shaped fin. The picture still wasn't enough to convince most scientists that Nessie is real.

Lots of people have tried to gather hard evidence of Nessie's existence. A small submarine has even explored the depths of the lake, but it had no luck. Perhaps Nessie and her family were hiding in an underwater cave. Or perhaps they swam out to sea to avoid detection.

Other Lake Monsters

Nessie isn't the only lake monster, though. Over 300 similar creatures have been reported in lakes in Africa, Australia, Canada, Russia, and the United States. In all cases, the lakes are cold, deep, and connected to the sea, just like Loch Ness.

Most of these lake monsters inhabit lakes in Scotland and Ireland. Twenty other Scottish lochs have their own monsters.

Here are some other well-known lake monsters from around the world:

- **Champ**, in Lake Champlain, Vermont
- **Manipogo**, in Lake Manitoba, Manitoba, Canada
- **Memphee**, in Lake Memphremagog, Vermont
- **Nahuelito**, in Nahuel Haupí Lake, Argentina
- **Ogopogo**, in Lake Okanagan, British Columbia, Canada
- **Storsjöodjuret**, in Lake Storsjön, Sweden
- **Tessie**, in Lake Tahoe, California

It seems as though every lake must have its own lake monster. It's more likely that local residents invented many of these monsters. A monster in the lake helps bring in tourists, who hope to catch a glimpse of the strange creature.

Living Dinosaurs

So many people have reported seeing lake monsters that scientists wonder if they might really exist. If so, what are they?

FUN FACT

Home Delivery

Ogopogo was known to the local Native Americans as N'ha-a-ith, a lake demon. They occasionally left it offerings of food in a cave that was believed to be its home.

Ready to Read/

Perhaps you might grow up to become a scientist who studies the oceans, like an oceanographer or a marine biologist. Get started right now with *Exploring the Oceans: Science Activities for Kids* by Anthony D. Fredericks (Fulcrum Publishing, 1998).

> Below the thunders of the upper deep;
> Far, far beneath in the abysmal sea,
> His ancient, dreamless, uninvaded sleep
> The Kraken sleepeth.

—From "The Kraken,"
by Lord Alfred Tennyson

Unfortunately, no physical evidence of these creatures has ever been found, so there is no way to prove whether Nessie and her cousins are real.

The most popular theory is that Nessie and the other lake monsters are living dinosaurs. The common description of all of these lake monsters matches the description of the **plesiosaur**. If this is so, the plesiosaur has survived over 65 million years without anybody knowing about it.

Scientists used to argue that Nessie couldn't be a living dinosaur because Loch Ness was too cold for a cold-blooded dinosaur to survive. New theories about dinosaurs suggest that they were warm-blooded, though. If this is true, then Nessie and her relatives could have adapted to the cold waters of the northern lakes.

The monsters don't *have* to be dinosaurs. Many other theories have been proposed. For example, an underwater wave called a **seiche** that moves back and forth in an enclosed body of water could make movements that could be mistaken for such creatures. A simpler explanation is that the lake

WORDS to KNOW

plesiosaur: a dinosaur that lived in the water. It had a broad body, long neck, short tail, and four large flippers for swimming. It lived between 250 and 65 million years ago. *Plesiosaur* fossils have been found on every continent in the world.

Everything Kids'

http://www.everything.com

To learn more about dinosaurs, visit some online dinosaur museums. My favorites are the Carnegie Museum of Natural History at *www.clpgh.org/cmnh/discovery*, the National Museum of Natural History at *www.nmnh.si.edu/paleo/dino,* and the Museum of Paleontology at *www.ucmp.berkeley.edu/diapsids/dinosaur.html.*

 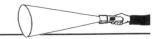

monsters are actually real animals—such as manatees, primitive whales, long-necked seals, giant otters, or overgrown eels—that were just misidentified. Short of draining the lake, though, it's impossible to prove that Nessie isn't a real monster.

Sea Monsters

Ever since people first set out to explore the ocean, they have told stories about the wondrous creatures that live in the sea. Many of those creatures we now know as whales, dolphins, and manatees. But many monsters also supposedly share the seas.

We have not completely explored the oceans. They are too big, and the weight of all that water makes it difficult for people to travel to great depths. Who knows what monstrous creatures lurk in the deep? We already know that the largest creatures on earth—whales—live in the oceans. Could there be even bigger creatures down there?

The oceans cover three-quarters of the earth's surface. Ninety-seven percent of the oceans are more than 600 feet deep, and the deepest trenches are 3,300 feet deep. That's a lot of room for a giant sea monster to hide in!

WORDS to KNOW

seiche: an underwater wave in an enclosed body of water, like a lake, that moves back and forth between the shores. The *seiche* (pronounced "saysh") could push logs or vegetation up to the surface, making it seem as if there are lake monsters. Loch Ness is an ideal location for such a wave.

kraken: a sea monster the size of a small island. Legends say that when the time comes for the world to end, the *kraken* will rise from the depths to devour every living creature in the sea.

Giant Squid and Octopi

The **kraken** is a legendary creature of Norse mythology that used to attack ships. Far larger than a whale, the kraken made a calm sea boil when it rose to the surface. It wrapped its many tentacles around ships, crushing them and dragging them beneath the waves.

WORDS to KNOW

cephalopods: a class of animals. *Cephalopod* means "head foot." All *cephalopods* have a group of arms around the front of their heads, called tentacles.

megalodon: an ancestor of the great white shark; *megalodon* means "giant tooth." The only fossils we have of this giant shark are its teeth, which can be as large as a person's hand and weigh more than a pound.

Creatures of the Deep

A variety of gigantic creatures live in the Antarctic region. Sea spiders grow up to 13 inches long there; sponges can grow up to 10 feet long; and there are 9-foot-long ribbon worms. It is so cold in the Antarctic that metabolic rates are lower, which enables the animals to get bigger and live longer than animals in warmer climates. Also, the Antarctic is very isolated, so there are fewer predators.

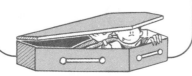

Now we know that the kraken is a real animal—the giant squid. No one believed that giant squid really existed until late in the last century, when the body of a dead giant squid washed up on shore.

Giant squid, from the class of animals called **cephalopods,** are true monsters. They can grow up to 100 feet long from their heads to the tips of their tentacles. We didn't discover the giant squid until recently because they live deep under the surface, nearly a half mile down, and they rarely surface. Fewer than fifty giant squid have been seen in the past century. Their only natural enemy is another giant of the oceans, the sperm whale. A giant squid may attack a ship if it mistakes the ship for a whale.

The giant squid might have a cousin, the giant octopus. This creature could grow up to 100 feet across and weigh ten tons. However, there is no reliable evidence that giant octopi exist. No giant octopus, living or dead, has ever been captured. Considering what we know about octopi, this is not unusual. Octopi are shy bottom-dwellers and rarely come to the surface. If they lived at the very bottom of the open ocean, we might never encounter them.

Giant Sharks

The largest creature and the greatest hunter ever to have lived was the **megalodon.** The megalodon ruled the oceans between 25 million and 1.6 million years ago. It was between 60 and 200 feet long. (The great white shark, the largest living shark, rarely grows more than 15 feet long.) The megalodon would have been big enough to swallow a car whole, and a whale would only have made a tasty snack.

In 1918, a group of Australian fishermen claimed to have had a close encounter with a huge shark that was much bigger than any shark they had ever seen before. There have been a

few other sightings of gigantic sharks since then, leading some people to wonder if the megalodon might have survived somehow. It is unlikely, because the oceans are now too cold for a megalodon.

Some people have theorized that the megalodon might still survive in the Marianas Trench, the deepest part of the Pacific Ocean. The waters of the Marianas Trench are warmed by volcanic activity. If the megalodon really did live that far down in the ocean, its metabolism would slow, and it would require less food. (It would probably eat giant squid!) But don't worry. Even if the megalodon did survive, it could never escape from the trench. The colder waters above would kill it.

What's Hiding in Loch Ness?

How many common words of three or more letters can you find hiding in the letters of LOCH NESS? Our scientists found fifteen, but there are even more than that! Use the following rules and see what you come up with.

- A letter may be used only as many times as it appears in the words LOCH NESS (so you can use S twice, but all the other letters only once).
- Proper names, abbreviations, and contractions are not allowed.

1. _____
2. _____
3. _____
4. _____
5. _____
6. _____
7. _____
8. _____
9. _____
10. _____
11. _____
12. _____
13. _____
14. _____
15. _____

Blow Monster Bubbles

When sea monsters, giant squid, and lake monsters come to the surface, they generally create a lot of large bubbles. You can make monster bubbles, too, using this simple recipe.

Ingredients
2 cups liquid dishwashing detergent
6 cups water
¾ cup light corn syrup
An old skillet
An old wire hanger

Directions
1. Mix the dishwashing detergent, water, and corn syrup together, and let it settle for about four hours.
2. Pour the mixture into an old skillet.
3. To make a bubble-blowing wand, bend an old metal hanger into any shape you like (the bubbles will all be round, though).
4. Blow very slowly and steadily to make bigger bubbles, or wave your wand through the air.

If you want to try making even bigger bubbles, mix up a batch of bubble solution in a plastic wading pool. Use a Hula-Hoop as your bubble-blowing wand. The biggest bubble ever blown was 50 feet long; maybe you can break the record!

CHAPTER 11
WEIRD CREATURES

WORDS to KNOW

cryptozoologists: people who study animals that have not been proved to exist. *Cryptozoologists* search for evidence of legendary monsters like Bigfoot, the Loch Ness Monster, and the weird animals described in this chapter. *Cryptozoology* is not a recognized branch of science.

El Chupacabra: Spanish for "the goat sucker." *El Chupacabra* got this nickname because it kills goats and other farm animals and then sucks their blood like a vampire.

Fearsome Animals

There are many strange animals. For instance, the duck-billed platypus is a mammal that has a duck's beak and webbed feet and lays eggs. Piranhas are fearsome fish that can pull a cow into the water and completely devour it within ten minutes. And the goliath bird-eating spider is a tarantula that actually hisses and is big enough to eat a bird. We know these animals exist. Scientists have studied them.

But several monstrous animals exist only in stories. Or do they? Perhaps they are so good at hiding that they have never been captured and studied. These animals are called "hidden creatures"; that is, they are animals that have not yet been discovered. **Cryptozoologists** search for these hidden creatures.

Q: Do monsters eat popcorn with their fingers?

A: No, they eat the fingers separately.

The most famous hidden creatures include *El Chupacabra*, the Jersey Devil, and the bunyip. All these creatures have been spotted in modern times, but no one has hard evidence that they are real.

El Chupacabra

The legends of **El Chupacabra** come from Puerto Rico and Central America. *El Chupacabra* stands between 3 and 4 feet tall and has glowing red eyes, long sharp fangs, and a row of spines down its back. It walks on its hind legs and has scrawny arms that end in claws. It smells terrible.

El Chupacabra eats goats, sheep, cows, and other farm animals. It kills them by slitting their throats and then drinking the blood. It has never attacked a person, though.

In 1995, several sightings of the monster were reported in Puerto Rico. More than 2,000 cases of animal

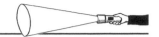

To learn more about this weird creature, visit the *El Chupacabra* Web site at *http://tlc.discovery.com/tlcpages/chupacabra/chupacabra.html*.

mutilation in Puerto Rico have been attributed to *El Chupacabra*. Since then, the sightings of this ugly monster have increased, and it has been seen in South America, Mexico, and the southern United States. Although there are lots of stories about the creature, there is no real evidence that it exists.

If *El Chupacabra* is real, what could it be? There are many theories. Perhaps it is a kind of dinosaur that managed to survive until today. Maybe it is a scientific experiment that somehow went wrong. It could even be an alien's pet left behind during a visit to Earth.

Most experts agree that there is no such thing as *El Chupacabra*. They attribute the livestock deaths to wild dogs or other animals.

The Jersey Devil

Stories about a hideous creature living in the isolated Pine Barrens area of New Jersey have been told since before the Revolutionary War. The creature is called the Jersey Devil. This monster has a head like a horse or a ram, curled horns, long thin wings like a bat, short legs, and cloven hooves. It stands 3½ feet tall and walks on its back legs. Its high-pitched scream would make any lone traveler hurry home. Seeing the Jersey

FUN FACT

Alien Happenings

Animal mutilations, particularly mutilations of cattle, are associated with aliens. In the 1970s, hundreds of cows were found dead in the western United States. Many of them had been drained of blood. At the same time, several UFOs were spotted in the area. That's why some people think *El Chupacabra* might be an alien of some kind.

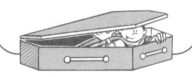

Where in the World?

The Pine Barrens area is located in the southeastern part of New Jersey. It covers 1.1 million acres, or 22 percent of the state. It was the country's first national reserve and is the largest tract of open land on the mid-Atlantic coast.

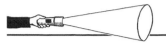

Devil was a sure sign of disaster to come. But until 1909, the stories were just legends.

In 1909, more than 100 people in thirty different towns reported seeing the Jersey Devil in the space of one week. A man walking along the electric railroad tracks reported the last sighting. He saw the Jersey Devil sniff the electrified rail of the tracks and then touch it with its long tail. There was a flash and an explosion, which melted 20 feet of the track, and the Jersey Devil disappeared.

Since then, the Jersey Devil has been rarely seen, and these reports might have been pranks or cases of mistaken identity. New Jersey residents have adopted the monster as the official state mascot, which is pretty special—not every state has its own monster!

The Bunyip

The bunyip is a bizarre creature that lives in rivers, swamps, creeks, **billabongs,** and other bodies of water in Australia. It is so monstrous and so rarely seen, that no one is quite sure what it looks like. Sometimes, it is described as having a flat face, scales, and a fish's tail. In other cases, it has a long neck, a beak, and a flowing mane. Or it may be a furry beast with a head like a bird. It can even look like a person with a horrible face and feet turned backward.

All of the stories agree on one thing: the bunyip's favorite snack is people. It also gives a bloodcurdling bellow that echoes throughout the swamp. The Aborigines, who have many stories about the bunyip, say it's an evil spirit that punishes the wicked and brings disease. In fact, the name *bunyip* is an Aboriginal word that means "demon" or "spirit." Today, the bunyip mostly appears in Australian children's books.

FUN FACT

The Devil State

New Jersey is proud to be the only state with its very own monster. The Jersey Devil was named the official state demon in 1939. New Jersey's NHL hockey team, the New Jersey Devils, is named after the monster.

billabong: a word used by the Aborigines, the Australian native people. *Billabong* refers to a still pool or a dry streambed that is filled with rain during part of the year.

Scared?

Do you know that there is a word that means "fear of monsters?"
Use this decoder to read the monster's eyes and see what the scary word is.

A B E H I O P R T

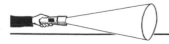 

Dragons

Stories about flying lizards, or **dragons,** are told throughout Europe, Asia, and North Africa. All dragons share several common characteristics. They are huge lizards with long fangs, and they usually have twin horns on their heads. Dragons have either scales or leathery skin and come in a wide range of colors, including red, green, black, and gold. All dragons can fly. European dragons have bat-like wings, whereas Asian dragons fly using magic.

All dragons don't look exactly the same. Some have one head; some have a hundred heads. Some have no legs, some have two, and some have four. Some can even breathe fire. Most dragons are very smart, though, and they usually have magical powers.

There are several different kinds of dragons:

- Asian dragons live in Asia and Indonesia.
- British dragons live in the United Kingdom.
- European dragons live in northern Germany, Scandinavia, and the islands of the North Atlantic.
- Mediterranean dragons live in Greece, Asia Minor, southern Russia, and northern Africa.
- Occidental dragons live in France, Italy, and Spain.

In Europe, dragons are considered fierce and evil. Great Britain has the most legends about dragons. Three kinds of dragons lived there: the fire-breathing Firedrake, the two-legged Wyvern, and the legless Worm. The medieval knights used to make a career out of killing dragons that were terrorizing the countryside. In Asia, however, dragons are considered friendly, and they bring good luck and fortune.

dragons: from the Greek word *draco,* which means "serpent." The constellation Draco got its name because it resembles a large *dragon.*

> **Q:** How do monsters tell the future?
>
> **A:** They read their horror-scopes.

Ready to Read?

Stories about the bunyip are popular in Australian children's books and have been told by the Aborigines for thousands of years. Read some of these stories for yourself in *Dreamtime: Aboriginal Stories* by Oodgeroo Noonuccal (Lothrop, Lee, and Shepard, 1994).

 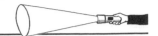
What Next?

This monster is growing eyes—and other parts, too! Figure out the pattern, then draw the correct number of eyes on the last head.

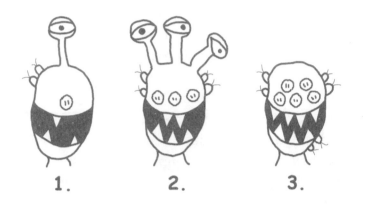

1.   **2.**   **3.**

> **66** My armor is like tenfold shields, my teeth are swords, my claws spears, the shock of my tail a thunderbolt, my wings a hurricane, and my breath death. **99**

—Smaug, the dragon in *The Hobbit* by J. R. R. Tolkien (Houghton Mifflin, 1973)

WORDS to KNOW

chimeras: from Greek mythology; a monster with the head of a lion, the body of a goat, and the tail of a dragon. *Chimera* now applies to any monster made up of parts of different animals.

Are there any real dragons? Not any that can fly. But a kind of dragon lives on a few tiny islands off the coast of Indonesia. They are called Komodo dragons and are the world's largest lizards. Westerners didn't discover Komodo dragons until 1910, but the native islanders have been telling stories about them for a long time. The Komodo dragon is another example of a weird creature that turned out to really exist.

Chimeras

Some hideous monsters are actually combinations of several different kinds of animals in one creature. These monsters are called **chimeras**. They are mostly characters in myths and legends, and none has been seen in modern times.

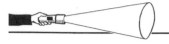

The Manticore

The manticore is a monster that lived in the jungles of Asia, particularly in India, Malaysia, and Indonesia. The manticore was a very dangerous predator. It had the body of a red lion but a head like a man with three rows of very sharp teeth. Its scaly tail was tipped with a ball of poisonous darts that it could fire like arrows at its victims. The manticore was very fast and could make powerful leaps.

Like many other monsters, the manticore liked to eat people. It devoured its victims completely, including their bones and clothing. Whenever someone went into the jungle and vanished, everyone knew that he or she had been eaten by a manticore.

Q: Why did the monster eat the tightrope walker?

A: He wanted a well-balanced meal.

Where in the World?

To locate Indonesia, first find the continent Australia, which is pretty much on the opposite side of the world from North America. Several groups of islands lay between Australia and southeast Asia, including Malaysia, Indonesia, and the Philippines.

Animal Instincts

The legend of the manticore may be based on real stories of man-eating tigers. Tiger attacks on people are rare, but they can happen as humans move into the tigers' habitat. Unfortunately, once tigers start killing humans, they usually don't stop and must be hunted and killed.

Create Your Own Monster

Make up your own monster to scare your friends and family. Think of three animals, preferably with some frightening characteristics. Combine them to make a completely new animal, your own chimera. For example, you might create a monster with the head of a wolf, the body of a tiger, and the tail of a crocodile. (I'd hate to run into something like that!) Draw a picture of what your new monster looks like. Come up with a good name for your monster, and write it beneath the picture.

Now, think up some details to make your monster really scary. Act as though you're a scientist and you've just discovered this new creature that you want to learn about. Try to answer some questions about it. For example:

Where does it live?
What does it eat?
Does it have any weapons, like poisonous fangs or spines coming out of
    its skin?
Is it dangerous to people?

Write down your answers to these questions and any other details on the picture of your monster.

_____

_____

_____

_____

_____

_____

_____

CHAPTER 12

ALIENS: THEY CAME FROM OUTER SPACE

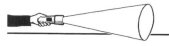 
Aliens among Us

Are we alone in the universe? Think about how big the universe is and how many planets there must be out there. It makes sense that life has developed on other planets. But how likely is it that alien life forms have built spaceships and flown across the vast distances of space to visit Earth?

Aliens have long been part of myths and legends. In ancient times, they were called by many names: angels, demons, fairies, and gods. They all shared common characteristics. Aliens came from some other place, usually the sky. They had awesome powers that regular humans didn't have. They were associated with flying ships or strange lights in the sky. And often, they meddled in human affairs.

Only in the present era, when we've flown rockets into space ourselves, have these nonhuman creatures been identified as aliens from a distant planet. In the modern world, we are fascinated with the possibility of exploring outer space and discovering life elsewhere in the universe. We are also afraid that alien life might be more technologically advanced and might try to take over Earth.

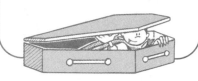

FUN FACT

Life in Space

According to biologists, 10 percent of the planets in the universe capable of producing life have done so. It is estimated that there are between 100 and 150 million planets in our galaxy, so there may be life on as many as 10 to 15 million planets. But "life" can mean something as small as bacteria or mold; it doesn't necessarily mean intelligent life capable of figuring out space travel.

Q: What did the astronaut cook for dinner?

A: An unidentified frying object.

Ancient Astronauts

Mysterious objects flying around the sky have been observed for at least 50,000 years. They appear in the stories and artwork of ancient peoples who knew nothing about space travel or rockets.

Some people believe that aliens have interfered with human history, guiding us through the stages of human evolution. This is called the Ancient Astronaut theory. According to this theory, aliens taught primitive

cultures math, astronomy, and even how to make batteries. Aliens were responsible for such marvels as the pyramids, the giant statues on Easter Island, and Stonehenge. Other people believe that aliens have merely been observing us for thousands of years, as if they were scientists and we were the experiment.

Modern-Day Sightings

The modern flying saucer craze began in 1947. A pilot named Kenneth Arnold was flying his plane near Mount Rainier in Washington State. He saw nine shining discs moving across the sky like saucers that "skipped across the water." When he reported this encounter, the phrase *flying saucer* was coined.

On July 4, 1947, the most famous event in **UFO** history occurred. During a severe thunderstorm, an alien spaceship crashed near Roswell, New Mexico. Several people witnessed the crash, and some even said that they saw bodies in the wrecked spaceship. The air force claimed that the "space-ship" was actually an experiment using high-altitude balloons that blew apart and fell back to earth. But all evidence of the crash was quickly hidden by the air force.

> **Q:** What is an alien's normal eyesight?
> **A:** 20-20-20

The "spaceship" and other evidence of the crash were whisked away to a secret air force base in Nevada called Area 51. This base is used to test top-secret military aircraft. Alien enthusiasts believe that the air force is developing flying saucer technology there by **reverse-engineering** the crashed flying saucer from Roswell.

After Kenneth Arnold's sighting and the crash at Roswell, a flying saucer craze swept the country. Flying saucers were spotted everywhere. Judging by all the reports, Earth must be the most popular tourist spot in the galaxy!

Where in the World?

Easter Island is one of the most isolated places on our planet. It is located in the South Pacific Ocean 2,000 miles from the coast of Chile. On your map, find Chile on the west coast of South America. Move your finger west into the Pacific to intersect Easter Island. Mysterious giant stone heads known as Maoi completely encircle the island on the coastline.

WORDS to KNOW

UFO: any object that is seen in the sky but that can't imme-diately be identified. *UFO* is short for *Unidentified Flying Object*. Although the term is usually synonymous with *spaceship*, it can also refer to planes, birds, and meteors.

reverse-engineering: the process of recreating something's design by looking at the final product. For example, if scientists ever found an alien spacecraft, they would take it apart to discover how it worked. Then they would try to make a new one just like it.

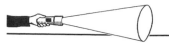 

Alien Adventure

If you like aliens, you can visit Roswell. The city has two alien museums and holds an annual festival called the UFO Encounter Festival during the first week in July. The festival features the world's largest parade of spaceships, puppet shows, costume contests, crafts, and laser light shows.

WORDS to KNOW

hypnosis: a state resembling deep sleep. Under hypnosis, a person might recover blocked memories. Hypnosis is used by many therapists to help people change their behavior like quitting smoking or getting rid of fears (like flying or going to the dentist).

Abducted!

Aliens weren't content to simply fly around the sky for long. They also wanted to study people close-up. Thousands of alien abductions, or kidnappings, have been reported, starting soon after Kenneth Arnold spotted those flying saucers.

One of the most famous abduction cases is that of Betty and Barney Hill. Their story is typical of most alien abductions.

In 1961, the Hills were driving late at night to their home in New Hampshire when a bright light descended toward them. They stopped their car and looked at the object with binoculars. They saw a saucer ringed with windows and colored lights hovering in the air. They could even see creatures standing inside. Two hours passed, but the Hills had no memory of what happened during that time.

Q: What did the alien say to the book?

A: Take me to your reader.

Soon afterward, Betty started dreaming that they had been taken aboard the saucer. She also began suffering from nervous breakdowns and ill health. She agreed to be hypnotized. Under **hypnosis**, she remembered going inside the spaceship and being examined by creatures with large, bald heads, almond-shaped eyes, and slit mouths.

The Mysterious Men in Black

Once a person has had a close encounter with an alien, he or she often reports a second strange encounter with mysterious men who dress all in black. These Men in Black—or, as they are often called, M.I.B.—usually show up before the victim even reports the alien encounter. The victim is generally alone when they arrive, so there are no witnesses to confirm the visit.

Who are the Men in Black? Are they government agents trying to keep accounts of alien visitors secret? Or are they aliens?

 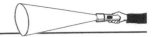
A Case of Mistaken Identity

In most cases, a UFO sighting can be explained. Around 95 percent of all UFOs can be identified after examining the evidence. Many natural phenomena can be mistaken for flying saucers, and lots of manmade objects occupy our skies.

The object most commonly mistaken for a UFO is the planet Venus. Other than the moon, Venus is the brightest object in the night sky. It usually appears in the early evening or predawn hours. Because it is so bright, and because it appears to move as Earth rotates, Venus can look like a spaceship flying far overhead.

The following have been mistaken for UFOs, as well:

- Airplanes, especially military planes
- Flocks of birds
- Meteors
- Orbiting satellites
- Reflections of light on clouds
- Rockets
- Space junk falling back to Earth
- Weather balloons

Strange natural phenomena have also been mistaken for UFOs, such as the northern lights, or *aurora borealis*. The northern lights appear during the dark hours in the polar regions of Siberia, Alaska, Canada, Greenland, Iceland, and Norway. Ball lightning, a rare form of lightning shaped like a ball that zips across the sky, can also look like a flying saucer.

Types of Aliens

In science fiction books and movies, aliens come in all shapes and sizes, ranging from "little green men" to tall, hairy Chewbacca in *Star Wars*. When people report encountering aliens in real life, the aliens also take many forms. Most alien descriptions fall into one of three distinct groups: Grays, Reptoids, and Nordics.

FUN FACT

UFOs?

During World War II, airplane crews on both sides reported strange lights and objects flying alongside their planes. Each side believed the objects were secret weapons being developed by the enemy. They were nicknamed "foo fighters" after a popular cartoon of the time. No explanation for these objects was ever found.

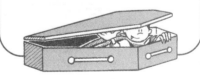

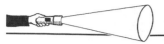

Grays

Grays are the most commonly encountered type of aliens. You're probably already familiar with what Grays look like from television or the movies.

Grays are generally short, between 3 and 4 feet tall. They have overlarge heads and thin, spindly bodies. Their smooth gray skin is what gives them their nickname. Their hands are webbed with four fingers. They have large, almond-shaped, dark eyes with no pupils. Other than that, Grays have no facial features, except for a tiny mouth like a slit.

Grays don't talk but perhaps communicate by telepathy. They seem very intelligent because of their large heads, but they show no emotion. They act like scientists, studying humans as we would study animal species.

Reptoids

Reptoids are reptilian creatures between 5 and 9 feet tall. They have powerful arms and legs with large muscles. Their four fingers are tipped with claws. Their skin is made of scales and is a greenish-brown color. Reptoids have large black eyes with vertical slits for pupils and two bony ridges on their heads. Sometimes they also have tails or wings.

Reptoids are highly advanced aliens, and some UFO researchers believe they are the rulers of the Grays. They are also very hostile to people, and they are the most

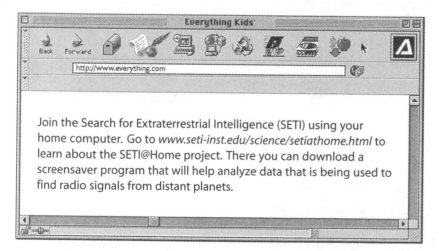

Join the Search for Extraterrestrial Intelligence (SETI) using your home computer. Go to *www.seti-inst.edu/science/setiathome.html* to learn about the SETI@Home project. There you can download a screensaver program that will help analyze data that is being used to find radio signals from distant planets.

dangerous of all aliens. According to the theories, they are plotting to overthrow our planet, and they might even eat people!

Nordics

Nordics are aliens that look human. They are 5 to 6 feet tall with blond hair and blue eyes. They are called Nordics because they look like the people of northern Europe. Their appearance matches the descriptions of other mysterious visitors recorded in legends and folktales, such as angels and fairies.

Nordics are supposed to be our friends. They are very peaceful aliens who try to help us against the more dangerous alien races. Because they look so much like human beings, some people believe Nordics are highly evolved humans who left earth a long time ago.

Ready to Read?

To read more about flying saucer crashes and alien abductions, accompanied by color photographs, get *Unexplained: UFOs and Aliens* by Colin Wilson (DK Publishing, 1997).

Aliens among Us

Halloween would be a perfect time for a real alien to check out Earth—who would notice? See if you can figure out who (or what) the real alien is in this group of trick-or-treaters.

a. Kelly is not the one with three antennae.
b. Both Ben and Lula have scales.
c. Mario is standing next to the alien with webbed feet.
d. Lula is not the one with two heads.

Go Skywatching

Skywatching is a fun hobby that you can do, even if you don't own a telescope. You only need a star map for finding objects in the sky. Because of Earth's rotation and orbit around the sun, the objects in the sky change during the night and at different times of the year. You can print out monthly star maps for free from *http://Skymaps.com* or buy a book of them in a bookstore.

Pick a clear, dark night for skywatching. Turn off the outside lights, if you can, or go to a dark place like a park or the countryside. Take binoculars to see objects close-up. Don't forget a notebook and a flashlight so you can record what you see. Before you go, visit *www.earthsky.com/Features/Skywatching/* for tips about what to look for that night. Even if you don't see any aliens, you're bound to see something interesting.

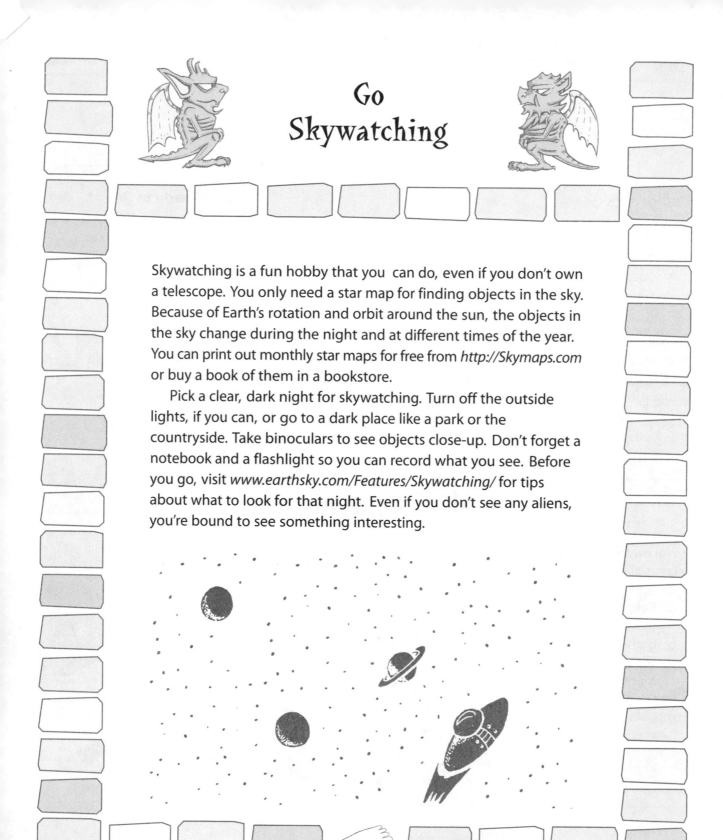

CONCLUSION

Why do we tell stories about monsters? To help understand the mysteries of the world we live in. To warn kids about what might happen if they don't behave. And to have fun getting just a little bit scared!

In this book, you've learned that monsters aren't always what they seem. Sometimes a real animal can be considered a monster until we understand what it really is. Sometimes we see monsters where there really is nothing—just stars in the sky or seaweed floating on the water.

Monsters live mostly in our imagination. There, we can make them do whatever we want. They can be frightening, or friendly. So don't stop looking for monsters or mysteries all around you. The world would be pretty boring without them!

66 All this visible universe is not unique in nature, and we must believe that there are, in other regions, other worlds, other beings and other men. 99

—Lucretius, a Roman philosopher who lived between 99 and 55 B.C.

APPENDIX A
RESOURCES

If you want to learn more about the monsters you read about in this book, I recommend the following books and Web sites.

Books

Baddriel, Ivor. *Fantastic Creatures: Investigations into the Unexplained* (Barron Juveniles, 1999).

Claybourne, Anna. *The Usborne Book of Ghosts and Hauntings* (Usborne Publishing, 2000).

Coburn, Broughton. *Triumph on Everest: A Photobiography* (National Geographic Society, 2000).

Cohen, Daniel. *Young Ghosts* (Scholastic Paperbacks, 1996).

Cross, Rubin. *Movie Magic* (Sterling Publications, 1996).

D'Aulaires' Book of Greek Myths (Picture Yearling, 1992).

De la Rosa, Sheila. *Ghost Files: Creepy . . . but True?* (Disney Press, 1997).

Dineen, Jacqueline. *Lift the Lid on Mummies* (Running Press, 1998).

Doyle, Sir Arthur. *The Supernatural Stories of Arthur Conan Doyle* (Random House, 2000).

English Fairy Tales (Everyman's Library Children's Classics, 1993).

Erdoes, Richard and Alfonso Ortiz. *American Indian Trickster Tales* (Penguin, 1999).

Fredericks, Anthony D. *Exploring the Oceans: Science Adventures for Kids* (Fulcrum Publishing, 1998).

Funston, Sylvia. *Monsters: A Strange Science Book* (Owl Books, 2001).

—. *Scary Science: The Truth Behind Vampires, Witches, UFOs, Ghosts, and More* (Owl Books, 1996).

Gelman, Rita Golden. *Vampires and Other Creatures of the Night* (Apple, 1992).

Hamilton, Jake. *Special Effects* (DK Publishing, 1998).

Heppelwhite, Peter. *Hauntings: The World of Spirits and Ghosts* (Sterling Publications, 1998).

Jenkins, Martin. *Vampires* (Candlewick Press, 2000).

Landau, Elaine. *The Loch Ness Monster* (Millbrook Press, 1993).

—. *Sasquatch: Man of the Woods* (Millbrook Press, 1993).

Mitton, Jacqueline. *Aliens* (Candlewick Press, 2000).

Noonuccal, Oodgeroo. *Dreamtime: Aboriginal Stories* (Lothrop, Lee, and Shepard, 1994).

Norman, Michael and Beth Scott. *Haunted America* (Tor, 1999).

—. *Historic Haunted America* (Tor, 1999).

Page, Jason. *Ghosts and Monsters* (Penguin, 2000).

Piper, Jim. *In the Footsteps of the Werewolf* (Copper Beech Books, 1996).

Walker, Paul Robert. *Bigfoot and Other Legendary Creatures* (Harcourt Brace, 1997).

Wilcox, Charlotte. *Mummies and Their Mysteries* (First Avenue Editions, 1997).

Wilson, Colin. *Unexplained: UFOs and Aliens* (DK Publishing, 1997).

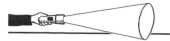 
Web Sites

Alien Encounters: *http://tlc.discovery.com/tlcpages/ encounters/encounters.html*

Aliens—Worlds of Possibilities: *http://exhibits. pacsci.org/aliens/welcome2.html*

The Bestiary on Eliki: *www.eliki.com/ancient/myth*

Bigfoot: *www.bfro.net*

Bigfoot—Fact or Fantasy?: *www.netcomuk.co.uk/ ~rfthomas/bigfoot.html*

Cryptozoology: *www.cryptozoology.com*

Cryptozoology: *www.thecryptozoo.com*

Dinosaurs: *www.clpgh.org/cmnh/discovery; www.nmnh.si.edu/paleo/dino*

El Chupacabra: *http://tlc.discovery.com/tlcpages/ chupacabra/chupacabra.html*

Encyclopedia of Monsters: *http://webhome. iderct.com/~donlong/monsters/monsters.htm*

Encyclopedia Mythica: *www.pantheon.org/ mythica*

Ghostly, Ghastly, Creepy, Crawly: *www. chirpingbird.com/netpets/html/features/oct/ ghostly1.html*

Ghosts—The Page That Goes Bump in the Night: *www.camalott.com/~brianbet/ghosts.html*

In Search of Giant Squid: *http://seawifs.gsfc. nasa.gov/squid.html*

Haunted Castle: *www.nationalgeographic.com/ castles/enter.html*

Jersey Devil site: *www.nj.com/jerseydevil*

The Legend of Nessie: *www.myspace.co.uk/nessie/*

Life Beyond Earth: *www.pbs.org/lifebeyondearth/ index.html*

Menacing Monster Guide: *www.factmonster.com/ spot/monsters1.html*

Monsters of the Deep: *www.abc.net.au/science/ ocean/monsters*

Mummies: *www.discovery.com/guides/history/ mummies.html*

Mummies Unmasked: *www.nationalgeographic. com/world/9906/mummies*

Mummies Unwrapped: *http://library.thinkquest.org/ J003409*

Museum of Unnatural Mystery: *www.unmuseum.org*

Nessie's Grotto: *www.simegen.com/writers/nessie*

Official Monster Hunter Site: *www.goldenbooks.com/ monsters*

Search for Extraterrestrial Intelligence: *www. seti-inst.edu/science/setiathome.html*

The Search for Monsters of Mystery: *www.nationalgeographic.com/world/ 9903/monsters*

Skywatching: *http://earthsky.com/Features/ Skywatching*

Star maps: *http://Skymaps.com*

A Study of the Golem: *www.scils.rutgers.edu/ special/kay/golem.html*

The Supernatural World: *http://library. thinkquest.org/27922/*

Trollmoon: *www.trollmoon.com*

Unseen Creatures: *http://library.thinkquest. org/27979*

Vampire party: *www.vamphalloween.com*

Voodoo: *www.voodoomuseum.com*

Werewolves: *www.tcfhe.com/goosebumps/ scary.html*

Y! Creature Catalogue: *www.yahooligans.com/ content/ka/almanac/creature/*

APPENDIX B
GLOSSARY

abominable snowman: The natives of Nepal call the yeti *meh-teh kangmi*, which means "man-like thing that is not a man." The first Western explorers incorrectly translated this to *abominable snowman*. Newspapers picked up the nickname, and it stuck.

anemia: From a Greek word meaning "without blood." *Anemia* can be caused by a disease or by poor diet. People with the most common form of *anemia* usually get better by eating foods that contain a lot of iron, like spinach.

archaeologist: A scientist who studies the remains of human cultures, such as fossils, artifacts, monuments, and *mummies*. *Archaeologists* try to figure out what the lives and beliefs of ancient peoples were like from what they left behind.

billabong: A word used by the Aborigines, the Australian native people. *Billabong* refers to a still pool or a dry streambed that is filled with rain during part of the year.

bogeyman: Any scary monster or person, or anything frightening that we don't know much about.

bokor: A sorcerer who practices both white magic and black magic. In *Voodoo*, white magic is done with the right hand and black magic with the left hand. So, a *bokor* is said to be someone who serves the lwa "with both hands."

bugbear or hobgoblin: Two other names for *goblin*. *Bugbear* and *hobgoblin* also mean anything that is difficult, frustrating, or frightening. For instance, you might say, "My math homework is a real *bugbear*."

camouflage: To disguise yourself so that you look like your surroundings. Because the Chenoo were made of stone, they could *camouflage* themselves by looking like the rocks around them.

canopic jars: Stone or ceramic jars specially designed to store the *mummy's* organs. The ancient Egyptians believed that anyone who could steal an organ from a *canopic jar* would gain the power to cast evil spells.

caul: A membrane, or thin skin, that may cover a baby's head at birth. The *caul* is simply pulled off the baby's head after birth. People used to think that babies born this way were supernatural or had magical powers.

cephalopods: A class of animal. *Cephalopod* means "head foot." All *cephalopods* have a group of arms around the front of their heads, called tentacles.

chimeras: From Greek mythology; a monster with the head of a lion, the body of a goat, and the tail of a dragon. *Chimera* now applies to any monster made up of parts of different animals.

cloning: Using a person's DNA to create another person who is identical to the first; the *clone* is like the original person's identical twin. Scientists may soon have the power to create human life through *cloning*.

Cronus: The Titan associated with time. Several English words related to time contain the prefix *chrono-*, which is derived from the name *Cronus*.

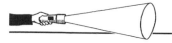 
cryptozoologists: People who study animals that have not been proven to exist. *Cryptozoologists* search for evidence of legendary monsters like Bigfoot, the Loch Ness Monster, and other weird animals. *Cryptozoology* is not a recognized branch of science.

decomposition: A natural process in which the body decays, or breaks down, after death. During *decomposition*, the skin changes color, the body swells, fluid leaks from the nose and mouth, and the fingernails and hair become loose. As a result, the hair and nails look as if they've grown.

dragon: From the Greek word *draco*, which means "serpent." The constellation Draco got its name because it resembles a large *dragon*.

ectoplasm: A slimy residue that ghosts leave behind. Mediums who are talking to ghosts may have *ectoplasm* come out of their noses and mouths.

El Chupacabra: Spanish for "the goat sucker." *El Chupacabra* got this nickname because it kills goats and other farm animals and sucks their blood like a vampire.

giant: From the word *gigantus*, which means "gigantic." A *giant* is a legendary human being of great size and strength who sometimes also has extraordinary powers.

goblin: From the Greek word *kobalos*, which means "rogue." A rogue is a dishonest, worthless, or mischievous person.

golem: A clay figure brought to life using holy magic. In the Jewish language of Hebrew, *golem* means "undeveloped lump."

gremlin effect: The tendency for things to go wrong at the worst possible time due to unexplained glitches.

haunt: From the same root as the word *home*. So, the place a ghost *haunts* is actually its home. In some areas, *haunt* is also another word for ghost.

Hebrew: The Jewish language. *Hebrew* uses a different alphabet than English, and it is written from right to left, instead of from left to right like English.

hoax: Something fake and often ridiculous that is passed off as real. *Hoax* probably comes from the word *hocus*, as in the phrase, *hocus pocus*.

holy water: Water that has been blessed by a Catholic priest. You can find holy water inside a Catholic church. The Catholic Church has fought vampires for centuries, which is why holy water and crosses are such good weapons against vampires.

hypnosis: A state resembling deep sleep. Under *hypnosis*, a person might recover blocked memories. *Hypnosis* is used by many therapists to help people change their behavior like quitting smoking or not being afraid of flying or of going to the dentist without fear.

inanimate: Not alive. An *inanimate* object cannot think for itself.

Kabbalah: Part of the Torah, or the body of Jewish holy writings. *Kabbalah* means "book of creation." It was written between 1,800 and 1,400 years ago.

knockers: One of the largest species of goblins, *knockers* have many different names depending on where they live. In northern Germany, they are called *kobolds*, and in southern Germany, they are called *wichtlein*.

kraken: A sea monster the size of a small island. Legends say that when the time comes for the world to end, the *kraken* will rise out of

 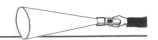
the depths to devour every living creature in the sea.

lunacy: Absence of normal or usual thought or actions. *Lunacy* comes from the Latin word *luna* for moon.

lycanthropy: From two Greek words: *lukos*, which means wolf, and *anthropos*, which means man. So, *lycanthropy* literally means "wolfman." People with *lycanthropy* can change into any kind of animal, though, not just wolves.

megalodon: An ancestor of the great white shark; *megalodon* means "giant tooth." The only fossils we have of this giant shark are its teeth, which can be as large as a person's hand and weigh more than a pound.

metamorphosis: A complete change of physical form, such as from a human being into a wolf, is called *metamorphosis. Metamorphosis* is usually accomplished by magic or other supernatural means.

mummification: The process of removing all of the moisture from a dead body. Because bacteria need water to survive, *mummification* keeps bacteria from invading the body and prevents it from rotting.

mummy: From the Arabic word *mumiyah*, which refers to a body preserved using wax. The term was incorrectly applied to Egyptian *mummies*, since they weren't preserved this way.

nosferatu: Another name for a vampire, *nosferatu* comes from a Greek word that means "plague-carrier." One of the first vampire movies was called *Nosferatu*.

odyssey: A long, adventurous journey. Odysseus was famous in Greek mythology for making a ten-year sea voyage and having many adventures along the way.

personification: An object or an idea that is given human form. For example, a giant who is the *personification* of the ocean might have hair made of seaweed and live at the bottom of the sea.

pharaohs: The kings of ancient Egypt. The word *pharaoh* means "one who lives in the palace." *Pharaohs* were believed to be a living link between humans and the gods.

phooka: A shapeshifting *goblin* that can appear as an animal like a dog, a bull, or an eagle. Its favorite form is a jet-black horse with blazing eyes.

plesiosaur: A dinosaur that lived in the water. It had a broad body, long neck, short tail, and four large flippers for swimming. It lived between 250 and 65 million years ago. *Plesiosaur* fossils have been found on every continent in the world.

poltergeist: The German word for "noisy ghost." Of all kinds of ghosts, *poltergeists* make the most noise and cause the most destruction.

psychic: Able to do extraordinary things with your mind, or a person who has that ability.

rabbi: The official leader of a Jewish congregation. A *rabbi* is also a master of Jewish law and religious teachings. He or she often acts as a teacher, passing knowledge along to others in the community.

reanimate: To bring a dead person or animal back to life, or make them appear alive again using magical or scientific means.

reverse-engineering: The process of recreating something's design by looking at the final product. For example, if scientists ever found an alien spacecraft, they would take it apart to discover how it worked. Then they would try to make a new one just like it.

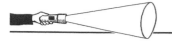 

sarcophagus: A stone coffin. Sometimes the *sarcophagus* was made of gold and silver. It was usually carved and painted to look like the person buried inside.

Sasquatch: Meaning "wild man of the woods." *Sasquatch* is the name given to Bigfoot by the native tribes of British Columbia, Canada. The legends of many Native American tribes mention Bigfoot.

scapegoat: Someone who takes the blame for mistakes or bad deeds committed by others. The term *scapegoat* comes from a biblical custom in which everyone's sins were symbolically placed on the head of a goat that carried the sins away into the wilderness.

schizophrenia: A disease of the brain. *Schizophrenia* often makes a person withdraw from reality. A person with *schizophrenia* may move slowly or clumsily, may not respond to others, and may not have any interest in life. All of these symptoms can be mistaken for the characteristics of a *zombie*.

seiche: An underwater wave in an enclosed body of water, like a lake, that moves back and forth between the shores. The *seiche* (pronounced "saysh") could push logs or vegetation up to the surface, making it seem as if there are lake monsters. Loch Ness is an ideal location for such a wave.

shamans: Priests, wizards, and healers of native tribes in Africa, North America, and Siberia. They are also known as "medicine men" or "witch doctors."

theory: A guess about something based on limited knowledge. Scientists come up with *theories* to explain what they don't understand, and then they conduct experiments to prove or disprove their *theories*.

titan: Someone of great size or strength, or someone who has done great things. The word *titanic* means huge. No wonder the largest cruise ship ever was named the *Titanic*.

UFO: Any object that is seen in the sky but cannot immediately be identified. *UFO* is short for *Unidentified Flying Object*. Although the term is usually synonymous with "spaceship," *UFO* can also refer to planes, birds, and meteors.

undead: A dead body that has been brought back to life, or *reanimated*, by a supernatural force. *Zombies* are also *undead* creatures.

Voodoo or Vodou: From the West African word *vodu*, which means "spirit" or "god."

were-beasts: Creatures that are half-man, half-animal. *Were-beasts* means "man-beasts." *Were* is an Old English word for "man." If you put the prefix *were-* in front of any animal's name, that means the animal is half-man.

will o' the wisp: A natural phenomenon, also called corpse candles, foxfire, and elf light. When pockets of swamp gas light up, perhaps due to spontaneous combustion of the gases given off by rotting plant matter, they form glowing blue balls of light that can look like ghosts.

zombie: From the African word *mzombi*, which means "spirit of a dead person." *Zombie* can also refer to a person who acts like a robot or shows no emotion or energy. If you don't get enough sleep at night, you may be a *zombie* in the morning.

zombify: To turn someone into a *zombie*. The entire process of changing someone into a *zombie* is called *zombification*.

PUZZLE ANSWERS

page 5 • **I Vant Your Vowels**

1. CR __E__ __E__ PY

2. FR __I__ GHTF __U__ L

3. GH __A__ STLY

4. GH __O__ __U__ L __I__ SH

5. SH __O__ CK __I__ NG

page 15 • **By the Light of the Moon**

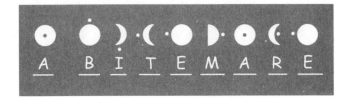

A B I T E M A R E

page 18 • **Ho-Ho-Howl**

		T		R	I	R		M		N		E	R						
A	E		C	H	E	L	V	I	S		S	I	H	E	S		A	D	S
W	N	R	E	H	T	I	E	T	R	I	M	A	N	D	V	C	L	C	L	S
O	T	O	N	W	O	H	S	E	F	A	H	G	V	A	S	E	K	I	W	A	U	S
W	E	R	E	W	O	L	V	E	S		H	A	V	E		C	L	A	W	S
O	N		T	H	E	I	R		F	I	N	G	E	R	S	–	K	I	D	S
A	T		C	H	R	I	S	T	M	A	S		H	A	V	E		C	L	A	U	S
		O	N		T	H	E	I	R		M	I	N	D	S	!			

page 26 • **Boo Who?**

These two faces are in Room 1, but not in Room 2.

This face is in Room 2, but not in Room 1.

page 29 • **Silly Séance**

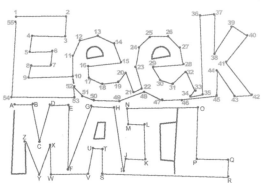

PUZZLE ANSWERS

page 30 • **I See a Ghost**

They get stage fright!

page 39 • **Come Back Here!**

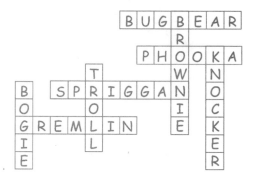

page 48 • **Crossing Guard**

doctor ~~frigid~~ ~~boots~~ (to) ~~nine~~
~~icy~~ (him) ~~wrong~~ ~~eleven~~ ~~clogs~~
~~baker~~ (told) ~~vintage~~ (bokor) ~~three~~
~~incorrect~~ ~~bizarre~~ ~~senior~~ ~~dancer~~
~~teacher~~ (the) ~~sandals~~ ~~aged~~
~~seven~~ ~~weird~~ ~~sneakers~~ ~~cook~~
~~peculiar~~ ~~odd~~ (because) ~~antique~~

Answer: Because the bokor told him to!

page 56 • **Mumbling Mummy**

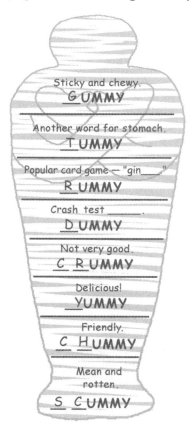

Sticky and chewy.
G UMMY

Another word for stomach.
T UMMY

Popular card game — "gin____."
R UMMY

Crash test _____.
D UMMY

Not very good.
C R UMMY

Delicious!
YUMMY

Friendly.
C H UMMY

Mean and rotten.
S C UMMY

page 58 • **Museum Mystery**

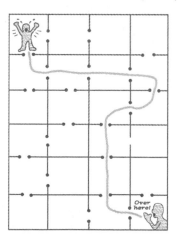

PUZZLE ANSWERS

page 66 • Basic Ingredients

1. Use **STONE** to create something that slithers.

   (switch 2nd and 4th letters, then change two letters) SNØXE SNAKE

2. Use **CEMENT** to make creatures that stand upright.

   (delete three letters) ¢ɆMENȾ MEN

3. Use **CLAY** to make a creature that lives in two shells.

   (change one letter) CLAɎ CLAM

4. Use **WOOD** to make a creature that howls at the moon.

   (change two letters) WOØXX WOLF

5. Use **ICE** to make creatures that squeak.

   (add one letter) MICE

6. Use **SNOW** to make a creature that flies in the night.

   (delete two letters, then add one letter) SXOW OWL

page 75 • Awesome!

```
    I M M E N S E
    C O L O S S A L
T R E M E N D O U S
      V A S T
G I G A N T I C
  T O W E R I N G
    E N O R M O U S
      H U G E
  M A S S I V E
```

page 77 • Super Sized

1. **IGB** BIG SHOT
2. **BMUOJ** JUMBO JET
3. **DAGRN** GRAND CANYON
4. **UPRES** SUPERMARKET
5. **NAITG** GIANT SQUID
6. **ERTGA** GREAT DANE

page 78 • The Big Picture

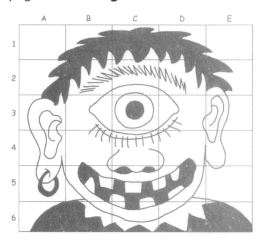

page 89 • Follow Those Footprints

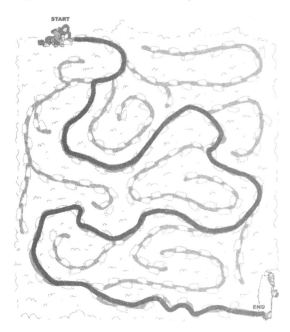

PUZZLE ANSWERS

page 91 • **Hink Pinks**

1. Nickname for a girl sasquatch named Elizabeth.

   Betty   Yeti

2. Cart used by a monster that breathes fire.

   dragon   wagon

3. Fake monster wrapped in linen.

   dummy   mummy

4. Just one big mean goblin.

   sole   troll

5. Serious monster made of clay.

   solemn   golem

page 99 • **What's Hiding in Loch Ness?**

Possible answers:

	HOLE(S)	LOSS
CHESS	HONE	NOSE(S)
CHOSEN	HOSE(S)	ONE(S)
CLONE(S)	LESS	SCONE(S)
CONE(S)	LESSON	SHOLE
ECHO	LONE	SHONE
HEN(S)	LOSE	SOLE(S)

page 105 • **Scared?**

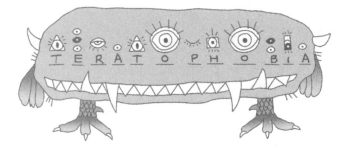

page 107 • **What Next?**

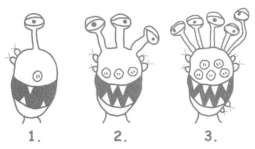

1.   2.   3.

Answer: In each step, add two more parts.

page 117 • **Aliens among Us**

Ben   Kelly   Alien   Mario   Lula

INDEX

A

Abominable snowman, 84–85
Alamo, 27
Alcatraz, 27
Aliens, 112–18
    abductions by, 114
    as ancient astronauts,
        112–13
    explanations of, 115
    Grays as, 116
    Nordics as, 117
    Reptoids as, 116–17
    reverse-engineering and,
        113
    Roswell, New Mexico and,
        113, 114
    sightings of, 113
    skywatching for, 118
    space life and, 112
    types of, 115–17
    UFOs and, 113, 114, 115,
        117
Anemia, 9
Archaeologist, 55, 56
Arnold, Kenneth, 113

B

Bathory, Elizabeth, 4
Bigfoot, 84–92
    animal track identification
        and, 92
    hoaxes, 88–91

names of, 84
    Sasquatch as, 85–86
    theories about, 87–88
    Web sites, 85, 88, 122
    Yeti as, 84, 85, 86–87
Billabong, 106–7
Black Dogs, 23
Bloody Countess, 4
Bogeyman, 31
Bogies, 38
Bokors, 44, 45–46
Boleyn, Anne, 26
Books, as resources, 121
Brownies, 36
Bubbles, monsters and, 100
Bugbear, 35
Bunyan, Paul, 77
Bunyip, 102, 104

C

Canopic jars, 54
Carter, Howard, 56–57
Catalepsy, 9
Caul, 7
Cephalopods, 98
Changelings, 36
Chimeras, 107
Clay monsters. See Golems
Clones, 68
Cronus, 72–73
Cryptozoologists, 102
Cyclops, 73–74

D

Decomposition, 3
Dinosaurs, 95–97
Dracula, 4–5
Dragons, 106–7

E

Easter Island, 113
Ectoplasm, 28
El Chupacabra, 102–3
Electro-Magnetic Field
    Detector (EMF), 27
Exorcism, 30, 31

F

Fairies, 34–35, 40
Flying saucers, 113, 117
Frankenstein, 68
Frost Giants, 74

G

Garlic, 2, 7, 8
Ghosts, 22–32
    Abraham Lincoln and, 27
    Black Dog, 23
    bogeyman and, 31
    contacting, 28–29
    defined, 22
    ectoplasm and, 28
    EMFs and, 27
    exorcising, 30, 31
    famous, 25–27

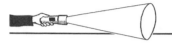 
Ghosts—*continued*
  finding, 24–27
  haunted house game and, 32
  haunted places and, 24–27
  history of, 22
  hopping, 49
  mediums and, 28
  poltergeists and, 30–31
  theories about, 23–24
  types of, 23
  Web sites about, 25, 122
Giants, 72–81
  in British folklore, 76–77
  defined, 72
  in Greek mythology, 72–74
  in Native American folklore, 80
  in Norse mythology, 74, 76
  ogres as, 80
  Web sites about, 76, 122
Giant sharks, 98–99
Giant squid, 98
Glossary of terms, 123–26
Goblins, 34–41
  bad luck and, 39–40
  brownies as, 36
  bugbear/hobgoblin, 35
  changelings and, 36
  defined, 34
  fairies and, 34–35, 40
  as practical jokers, 35–36
  protection from, 40
  types of, 36–39
  Web sites about, 35, 122
Gogmagog, 77

Golems, 62–69
  as attackers, 65–67
  defined, 62
  eliminating, 67
  Frankenstein and, 68
  history of, 62–64
  Kabbalah and, 64
  making, 64–65, 69
Grays, 116
Gremlins, 36, 37

H
Halloween costumes
  goblin, 41
  vampire, 10
Haunted places, 24, 25
Hebrew, 64, 65
Hobgoblin, 35
Holy water, 7, 8
Hypnosis, 114

I
Imagination, 119
Inanimate objects, 67

J
Jersey Devil, 102, 103–4

K
Kabbalah, 64
King Tut, 56–57
Knockers, 38
Kraken, 97–98

L
Lake monsters, 94–97
Lincoln, Abraham, 27

Lobisòn, 13
Loch Ness Monster, 94–95
Loew, Rabbi Judah, 63–64
Lunacy, 19
Lwa, 44–45
Lycanthropy, 12, 19
Lycaos, 15

M
Manticore, 108
Mediums, 28
Megalodon, 98–99
Men in Black (M.I.B.), 114
Metamorphosis, 14, 15
Monsters, creating, 109
Monster stories, writing, 81
Moon, 19, 20
Mummies, 52–59
  accidental, 52–53
  apple, making, 59
  curses of, 55, 56–57
  defined, 52
  Egyptian, 53–54
  making, 54–55
  Titanic and, 58
  Web sites about, 52, 122
Mummification, 52, 54–55

N
Nordics, 117
Nosferatu, 2

O
Octopus, giant, 98
Odyssey, 73
Ogres, 80
Ouija board, 29

P

Personification, 74
Pharaohs, 54
Phookas, 36, 37
Plesiosaur, 96
Plogojowitz, Peter, 3
Poltergeists, 30–31
Psychic powers, 23, 24
Puffer fish, 47
Puzzle answers, 127–30

R

Rabbis, 62, 63
Reanimation, 44
Reptoids, 116–17
Resources, 121–22
Reverse-engineering,
    113

S

Sarcophagus, 55
Sasquatch. See Bigfoot
Scapegoats, 39
Schizophrenia, 47
Sea monsters, 97–99
Seiche, 96, 97
Shamans, 12
Shapeshifters, 12–14. See
    also Werewolves
Sharks, giant, 98–99
Shelley, Mary, 68
Skywatching, 118
Spirits. See Ghosts
Spriggans, 38–39
Squid, giant, 98
Stoker, Bram, 4–5, 8
Stubb, Peter, 15–16

T

Tepes, Vlad, 4–5
Titans, 72–73
Tower of London, 25–26
Tricksters, 35–36
Trolls, 37–38

U

UFOs, 113, 114, 115, 117
Undead creatures, 6

V

Vampires, 2–10
    blood-drinking, 4, 6, 7
    as costumes, 10
    diseases and, 9
    Dracula and, 4–5
    garlic and, 2, 7, 8
    history of, 2–5
    holy water and, 7, 8
    powers of, 6
    preventing/killing, 7, 8
    real-life, 4–5
    today, 5–6
    turning into, 7–8
    Web sites about, 8, 122
Voodoo (Vodou), 44–49

W

Web sites, 122
Were-beasts, 13
Werewolf Syndrome, 16
Werewolves, 13–20
    biting capacity of, 17
    defined, 13
    first, 14–15
    history of, 13–16

identifying, 16–17
    moon and, 19, 20
    shapeshifting and, 12–14
    trials of, 15–16
    turning into, 17–19
    Web sites about, 14, 17, 122
Will o' the wisp, 23
Winchester, Sarah, 26–27

Y

Yeti, 84, 85, 86–87

Z

Zombie powder, 47
Zombies, 44–50
    banning, 44
    black magic and, 45
    Bokors and, 44, 45–46
    curing/preventing, 47
    defined, 44
    duppy, 46
    honoring ancestors and, 50
    making, 46–48
    movie, 48–49
    puffer fish and, 47
    schizophrenia and, 47
    servant spirit, 45
    Voodoo and, 44–49
    Web sites about, 45, 122
Zombify, 46

THE EVERYTHING®  KIDS' SERIES!

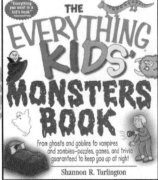

Packed with tons of information, activities, and puzzles, the Everything® Kids' books are perennial bestsellers that keep kids active and engaged. Each book is 8" x 9 ¼", 144 pages, and two-color throughout.

All this at the incredible price of $6.95!

The Everything® Kids' Cookbook
1-58062-658-0

The Everything® Kids' Monsters
1-58062-657-2

The Everything® Kids' Baseball Book, 2nd Ed.
1-58062-688-2

The Everything® Kids' Joke Book
1-58062-686-6

The Everything® Kids' Mazes Book
1-58062-558-4

The Everything® Kids' Money Book
1-58062-685-8

The Everything® Kids' Nature Book
1-58062-684-X

The Everything® Kids' Puzzle Book
1-58062-687-4

The Everything® Kids' Science Experiments Book
1-58062-557-6

The Everything® Kids' Soccer Book
1-58062-642-4

The Everything® Kids' Travel Activity Book
1-58062-641-6

Trade Paperback, $12.95
1-58062-147-3, 304 pages

The Everything® Bedtime Story Book

by Mark Binder

The Everything® *Bedtime Story Book* is a wonderfully original collection of 100 stories that will delight the entire family. Accompanied by charming illustrations, the stories included are retold in an exceptionally amusing style and are perfect for reading aloud. From familiar nursery rhymes to condensed American classics, this collection promises to promote sweet dreams, active imaginations, and quality family time.

The Everything® Mother Goose Book

by June Rifkin

The Everything® *Mother Goose Book* is a delightful collection of 300 nursery rhymes that will entertain adults and children alike. These wonderful rhymes are easy for even young readers to enjoy-and great for reading aloud. Each page is decorated with captivating drawings of beloved characters. Ideal for any age, *The Everything*® *Mother Goose Book* will inspire young readers and take parents on an enchanting trip down memory lane.

Trade Paperback, $12.95
1-58062-490-1, 304 pages

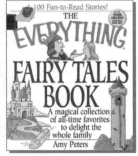

Trade Paperback, $12.95
1-58062-546-0, 304 pages

The Everything® Fairy Tales Book

by Amy Peters

Take your children to magical lands where animals talk, mythical creatures wander freely, and good and evil come in every imaginable form. You'll find all this and more in *The Everything*® *Fairy Tales Book*, an extensive collection of 100 classic fairy tales. This enchanting compilation features charming, original illustrations that guarantee creative imaginations and quality family time.

Available wherever books are sold!
To order, call 800-872-5627, or visit us at everything.com

Everything® is a registered trademark of Adams Media Corporation.